Montivagus Press, the imprint of Montivagus Productions, LLC
www.montivaguspress.com

First Edition 2021

HEY! I'M TALKIN' HERE.

The Story Behind
the Hit Comedy Documentary
I'm No Dummy

Bryan W. Simon
with Marjorie Engesser

Montivagus Press the imprint of Montivagus Productions

Foreword

Our history, heritage, enlightenment, culture and even entertainment is shared through stories. But, like telling a good joke, not everyone can tell a good story.

A good story is not just a matter of stringing a bunch of interesting facts, situations and characters together; to be compelling, a GOOD story has to capture your imagination. Throughout centuries of telling stories, good story tellers refined their methods and found better ways to tell tales. A good story combines creative structures and compelling presentations. When the story is presented as a film, structure becomes even more important as it involves the spoken word and images. In the case of a film documentary, structure, detail and presentation are everything and directing a film documentary can sometimes be a matter of frame by frame choices. That said, the magic of telling a good story has to be invisible to the audience. If you see the wires you can't really believe the magician is floating the lady.

If, like me, you are fascinated by the backstage view of a magic trick, this is the book for you. Director Bryan W. Simon explains frame by frame all the decisions and tricks he used to present his compelling film documentary on the art of Ventriloquism…*I'm No Dummy.* In addition to being a good film director and accomplished story teller, Bryan is also an excellent teacher as you will find out from reading this book. The story "hardscape" which Bryan explains is true, not just for a documentary on ventriloquism, but the blueprint of every good story. If you have seen *I'm No Dummy,* you will be amazed by what you didn't see. If you haven't seen the film, you will understand why *I'm No Dummy* is a fascinating story.

Enjoy the read,

Jay Johnson

Introduction

Making movies is difficult, if not nearly impossible. I've been fortunate enough to make a handful of films and every experience was similar, yet different and unique.

This book is a way to provide an enhanced and expanded transcription of the original director's commentary for my documentary *I'm No Dummy*. My audio commentary is only on the two-disc special edition DVD set that was released in 2015, so this book is for you streamers.

My director's commentary pulls back the curtain on how this particular film was made. I enjoy the "craft" of filmmaking as well as the unexpected deeper insights I learn through the process of making a film. Many of those are here. I hope this director's commentary opens your eyes to what I saw and takes you "behind the scenes" of this documentary.

On the DVD, my commentary occasionally paused to allow a significant moment in the film to surface. In this book, the person on camera is noted in [brackets]. Also included are photos which illustrate the point, but obviously are not part of the documentary itself. In some sections, there are stills that mark where we are in the film, but have no relationship to what I am speaking about.

Enjoy and thanks,
Bryan W. Simon

Hi, I'm Bryan, the director of *I'm No Dummy*, and it appears that you've clicked on the wrong menu button and you are listening to my director's commentary. I'm glad you're here. As we get through these company logos, I want to thank Tim Miller and my wife Producer Marjorie Engesser, they are my partners in Montivagus Productions; Cinematographer Lloyd Freidus and Doug Zwick of Pop Twist Entertainment.

You'll notice there are only two title cards here. I like to get into my films right away and use end title cards. I've done that on almost all of my films.

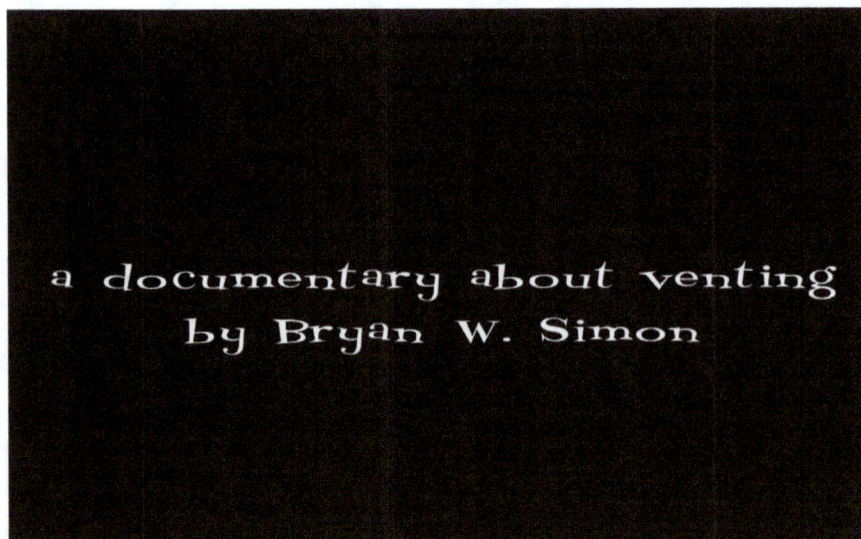

a documentary about venting
by Bryan W. Simon

This opening segment or teaser is really a tip of the hat to an idea that I had, and ultimately abandoned, after shooting a couple of interviews with the ventriloquists and their partners. I wanted to do interviews with the figures themselves, that is, no ventriloquists on screen or in the frame. It sounded like a really good idea, but it just didn't work.

First, puppets often have a singular and distinct personality, so if they were a confrontational or angry puppet, every answer would be angry or if they had a timid personality, they wouldn't want to talk to me. This may sound odd but they really must be separate beings for the illusion to work. Secondly, a lot of the emotion

Lamb Chop

that we get from the puppet can often be a reflection, in some ways, of how the ventriloquist reacts to that puppet. So having the vent on screen with the puppet was often necessary. But for this sequence, I solved the problem by having puppets saying the title of the film, and mixing in some clips. This gave us visual and musical signification that we will have fun, see something in a new light, and perhaps learn a thing or two. So there you have it. I think it was an entertaining and interesting way to start.

The music for the film was composed by Elliot Anders. He did a terrific job taking what I heard in my head and putting musical notes to it. I wanted something fun, light, whimsical with a dash of Warner Brothers cartoon added in for good measure. That's exactly how I described it to him and it was a very easy music collaboration.

Bob and Jay Johnson

This first section is entitled "What's Ventriloquism?" and the object was to have ventriloquists and their partners describe what ventriloquism was to them, and then illustrate those comments in the form of clips. We shot most of the people we interviewed in their homes, as you can see here with Jeff Dunham. And then the rest at the Vent Haven Ventriloquist ConVENTion.

Walter and Jeff Dunham

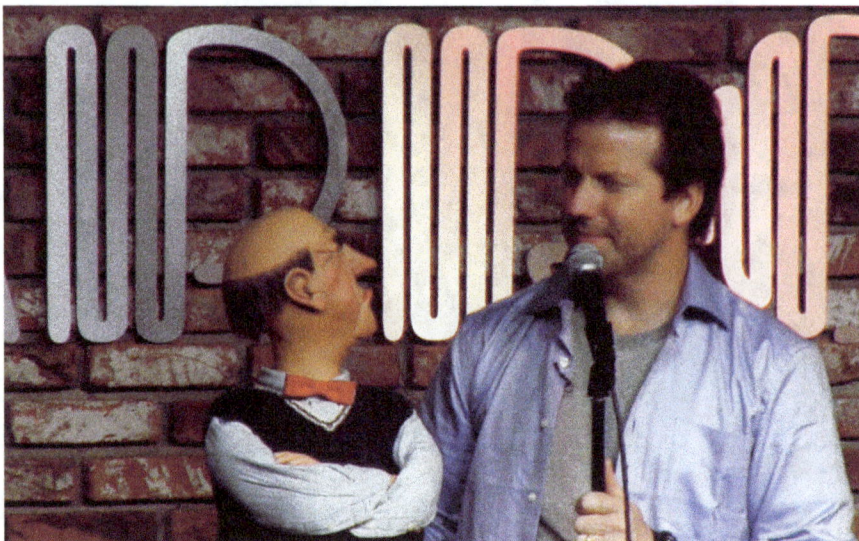

Walter and Jeff Dunham

The first performance clip of Jeff Dunham was shot at The Improv in Irvine, California. This was the first of several performances that we filmed of Jeff. We actually shot his performances in four different locations. Each venue was larger than the previous one. As we were shooting the doc, his popularity was increasing rapidly and unexpectedly.

This is Mallory Lewis and Lamb Chop. Lamb Chop was actually Shari Lewis' partner. Shari was Mallory's mom and Mallory is the only ventriloquist that I know of that continued an established character. Puppets or dummies can change hands, but there's an unwritten rule in the vent world that when a vent dies, the character or personality is retired as well. Mallory chose to have Lamb Chop live on, which was a bit controversial in the vent community. Also Lamb Chop's personality has changed now that Mallory has performed with the puppet for awhile.

Lamb Chop and Mallory Lewis

What's ventriloquism? This was the first question I asked every person we interviewed and there are a wide variety of interesting answers.

For Jay Johnson, it was about acting and reacting within the same word as well as the same scene.

For Jeff Dunham, it was about the comedy and making people laugh.

For Lynn Trefzger, it was a way of expressing different sides of her personality.

Camelot and Lynn Trefzger

And museum Curator Lisa Sweasy's take is that ventriloquism is a monologue perceived as a dialogue. I was surprised at the thoughtful and very personal answers that were given.

We shot this footage of Jay Johnson and Bob at Mike Lacey's Comedy and Magic Club in Hermosa Beach, California. It opened in 1978 and has become one of the great comedy clubs in the world. Many of the best comedians of all time have performed there. On several occasions, I shot a second camera with Lloyd. This angle I shot at the club because I knew exactly what I wanted it to look like. It is a called a dirty two shot. I wanted to focus our attention on Bob, but make sure that we see Jay, for the reasons I mentioned before about not having the puppet alone on screen.

Bob and Jay Johnson

Why did I choose a subject like ventriloquism for my first documentary?

I am not a ventriloquist. I don't speak without moving my lips, I've never owned a puppet, so it does beg the question: "Why Ventriloquism?" when there are a million other subjects that could be explored.

Luis Buñuel

I always got a kick out of that art form. It brings out that eight-year-old boy in me. I am a surrealist at heart, deeply influenced by Spanish filmmaker Luis Bunuel and Spanish artist Salvador Dali and I think the mere act of ventriloquism is pretty surreal.

I thought I could examine two very interesting themes: is it an art form or just a novelty act? And, is it dead? I love the idea of deconstructing film and so deconstructing this art form was particularly interesting to me. And I liked the idea of a comedy doc. I'm a student of comedy and that aspect of ventriloquism intrigued me.

Salvador Dali

I came up with the idea of *I'm No Dummy* on a bicycle ride. I was trying to come up with a simple and creative idea for a feature film because a writer's strike had stalled all of our other projects. I needed something that could be easily shot and I figured a documentary might just fit the bill. So while I was riding back to our place, I was thinking, "What could this doc be about that I have an interest in?" I thought – ventriloquism.

Martha McHaggis and Mary Kingsley

When I got home from that two-hour bike ride I told my wife, Producer Marjorie Engesser, about my idea and we did a little research. I thought for sure that there would be 10 or 15 feature length docs about ventriloquism, and you know what? There wasn't a single one. Not one. Only a couple of short docs that never really saw the light of day and some segments on news magazine TV shows. So we figured OK, lets do this. Shortly thereafter *I'm No Dummy* became the first feature length documentary about ventriloquism.

Other than a couple of quick clips in that intro section this is the first section of the documentary that has lengthy clips and photos. On the surface it may seem like there's nothing to discuss in that regard. But there is and it's a big deal.

Ronn Lucas

One of the biggest challenges to making a documentary is being able to afford all of the supplemental materials like clips and photos that you need to illustrate the ideas of your film. Many filmmakers are turning away from documentaries like this and choosing a more narrative style to avoid those costs.

When I first started doing research I spoke with a documentarian who told me the going rate for film or TV clips was about one hundred dollars a second, with a nine second minimum. That means a ten second clip is one thousand dollars. I thought my idea was over, before I had even started. But then, and I can't remember how, it occurred to Tim, Marge and I to speak with attorney Michael Donaldson and his partner Lisa Callif in Beverly Hills, California. Donaldson and Callif are known for their expertise in fair use doctrine. Without fair use, *I'm No Dummy* would never have been made.

So what's fair use?

Fair use grants you the ability to use copyrighted clips and photos in your documentary. The idea is that if you are judicious in your use of a copyrighted work then you can use it to illustrate your point. For this film, we would use short clips or photographs to help get our point across to the viewer. In order to utilize fair use properly, you need a very knowledgeable lawyer like Michael Donaldson or Lisa Callif to guide you through.

We shot a lot of performance footage. Jeff Dunham, Jay Johnson, and Lynn Trefzger we shot ourselves, but Ronn Lucas and much of the archival footage was material they provided or came from a collector or some other source.

Jerry Mahoney and Paul Winchell

[Lisa Sweasy] *"To me, it's a monologue that has to be perceived as a dialogue or it's no good."*

Lisa Sweasy

Theo and Stevo Schüling

[Stevo Schüling] *"Very much a focus through which I see our life and times."*

We interviewed Dr. David Goldblatt, a non-vent, about the art form. You'll see and hear him several more times in the film. Dr. Goldblatt wrote a book entitled *Art and Ventriloquism*. It was a scholarly treatment using the act of ventriloquism as a metaphor for all art forms. It examines how the relationship between ventriloquist and dummy works the same for the artist, the artwork, and the audience in regards to artistic intentions. When a filmmaker or artist is asked "What's the meaning?" The artist will often respond "It speaks for itself."

Dr. David Goldblatt

Here's a fascinating short piece of his interview that I wasn't able to fit into the documentary:

[Dr. David Goldblatt] *"We begin to see this kind of conversational exchange in the separation of one's self from a work. So we often say 'what does the work say to you,' and yet we know that the work is an inanimate object and we know that we're there by ourselves. And so the idea of interpretation, which some people would say is really definitional of an art work, is really a matter of a kind of ventriloquial exchange with the work. The more we know about the work the more the work says to us, the more we are able to say in some sense, back to it. And I think that there are, I am using voice here, vocality, also as part of this metaphor but there are obvious works – literature, poetry, music – in which there are actually, really are sounds. So there's a kind of phonetics here, that we are talking about in terms of voice."*

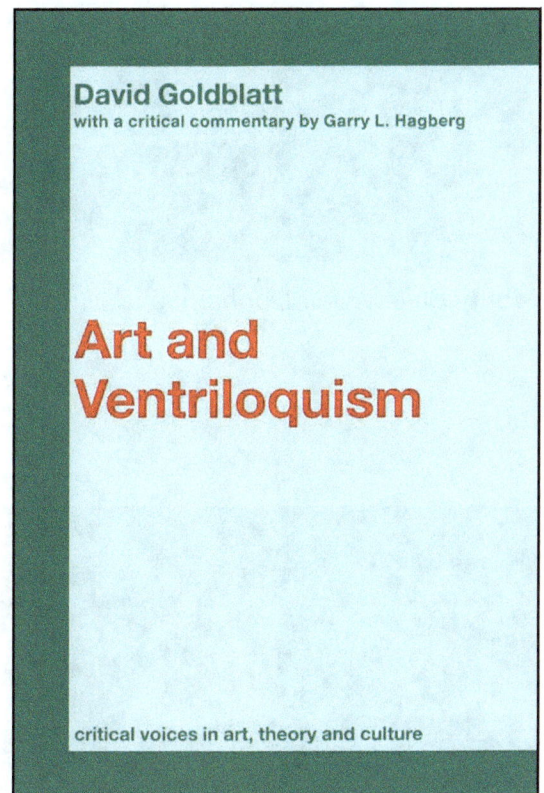

David Goldblatt
with a critical commentary by Garry L. Hagberg

Art and Ventriloquism

critical voices in art, theory and culture

This resonates with me as a filmmaker because I am expressing myself, and my thoughts, about this art form through it. I find it so important that we have an art form that in some ways is the metaphoric basis for all other art forms. That makes the act of ventriloquism pretty darn important to me.

Why vent?

Why ventriloquists vent was a revelation to me because I didn't automatically know what the answer would be. Their answers were very similar: they were shy, started primarily before puberty, got some recognition and support for their talents, but if they excelled at sports or were very popular for another reason, they often abandoned the art. However, if they made a few dollars and saw this as a talent that they could uniquely master, they continued into their adulthood with varying degrees of success.

Monty Ballew, Jeff Dunham, and Jimmy Nelson

There were so many stories that the ventriloquists shared with us. You have to remember we spent hours filming each and every one of them. We had over 150 hours of footage, an average of three hours for every person. One of the stories I really found compelling but could not include in the doc was from Lynn Trefzger. I could tell you that story, but I'm going to have her do it:

Emily and Lynn Trefzger

[Lynn Trefzger] "Well, I was still doing shows, I was still performing, but I didn't want my friends to know because I was afraid that they didn't think it was cool. I was a cheerleader, I was doing track and things like that so I was pretty well rounded, but I did do shows, I just didn't tell people, my friends, that I was doing them. There was point in my life when I was about 12 or 13 that I was doing volunteer work at the hospitals, I was doing shows at hospitals. And my mom, who was never a stage mom, whenever she would get a phone call for me to perform she would never take it unless I came home from school, and she would ask if I wanted to do it. Now she's raising eight kids, my mom and dad, they would have to rearrange their whole schedule just for my little hobby. But I remember this one time, I had to go do a hospital show and I was just like, oh, I don't want to, there's a softball game and I'm missing my softball game. She said, 'Lynn, you know you took this, so you have to do it.' So I went there and I was

Simon, Lynn Trefzger, and Honeybunch

just in a bad mood and I got to the hospital and while I was doing my show, my mood eventually changed. I would do my little show and then afterwards, I would walk around with my puppet and talk to the patients. I got to this one little girl, she was about nine years old, and the puppet's going back and forth talking to her and she's into it. All of a sudden all these doctors and nurses are standing around crying, just crying and I'm thinking what did I do. Apparently she was shot in the back accidentally, so she was paralyzed and she's been there for about a month or so, and has not spoken at all. This is the first time she opened up. So I think right there it kinda clicked. It's like, wow, she's just talking to the puppet. She wasn't talking to me, she was talking to my dummy so I think that's when it kinda clicked that this is pretty cool. I can keep on doing this, so ever since then my attitude changed about this."

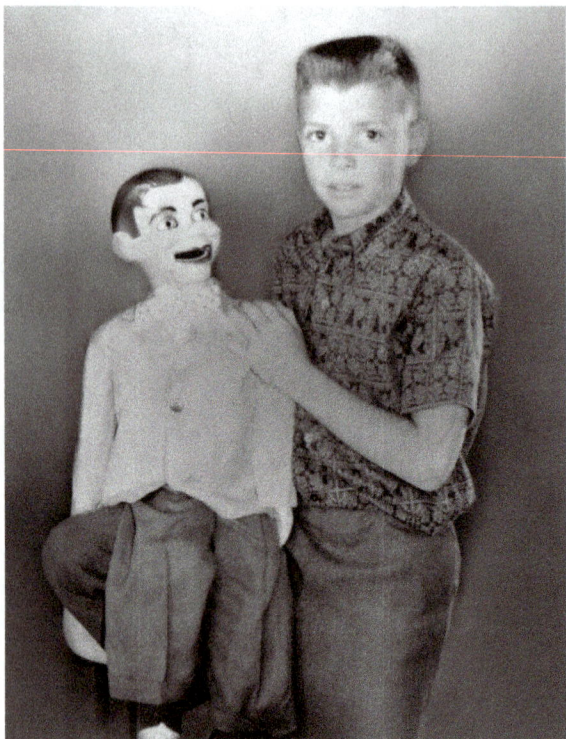

Squeaky and Jay Johnson

That story perfectly illustrates those watershed moments that many of these vents had. Every successful ventriloquist is successful because they found something that worked for them, and the recognition and satisfaction from it.

Willie Tyler and Lester were my first vent and partner interview and I thought it would be really easy to interview a puppet. But I gotta tell you, it was hard. It was difficult to see the puppet as a person that close up. I was only a couple of feet away. But after awhile, I settled in and from then on, I had no problem having an exchange with the figure.

On *Late Night With David Letterman*, Willie and Lester performed the hambone. The hambone is a musical technique that uses the human body as an instrument. You can slap your

Willie Tyler

thighs, your knees, your chest, anywhere on the body to make a sound. Willy takes the hambone and brilliantly combines it with ventriloquism.

I was told by another documentary filmmaker that you can't be friends with your subjects. I agree and disagree. I agree, because a couple of ventriloquists were upset that they didn't appear

Lester and Willie Tyler

in the film and one was upset that she was only in it a little bit. I disagree, because I did however make some very good friends that I know will be a part of my life forever. Those were the ones that were as proud of the film as I was and understood what it takes to pull off something like this.

One clip of Jay Johnson at the Comedy and Magic Club never ceases to amaze me. Jay doesn't do stand up in a traditional way. It is very character driven, which means it takes several minutes or more to get to the punch line. That made for some difficult cutting because I wanted to keep clips around a minute or so. Not just for fair use concerns, but to keep the documentary moving. Illustrate the point and move on. I love the way Jay can design a comedy bit around conjugating a verb. It's really something to see; that rapid-fire exchange

between the ventriloquist and his partner. That rapid-fire technique *Bob and Jay Johnson* was not invented by Jay, but how he adapted it for himself and his character, is what makes him a comic genius. You will see this time and time again with all of these ventriloquists as they take something they've seen and then make it their own.

"Don't Move Your Lips!" starts off with a clip that I think wonderfully shows what bad ventriloquism is from one of the best sitcoms ever produced, *The Dick Van Dyke Show*. I saw it in syndication when I was young and I still watch it today. I think it is as good as any modern day sitcom. It is brilliant and I can't tell you how much I was influenced by this TV show.

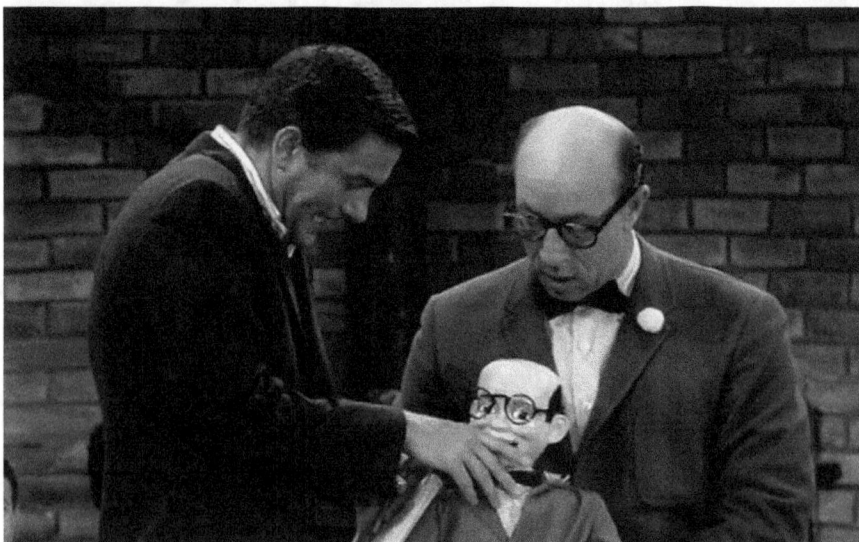

As a student of comedy, growing up in Waukegan, Illinois, I learned so much watching these ventriloquists work. I acquired a new level of understanding from the amazingly talented ventriloquists I saw while filming.

The Dick Van Dyke Show, October 10, 1963, "Too Many Stars"

Great vents all have several things in common. They make the DECISION to follow this path or dream. It's first a DECISION. They have a deep sense of COMMITMENT to their craft. They are going to stick with it through thick and thin; a single minded focus in pursuit of that goal and finally they have an UNDERSTANDING that they must find the one thing that not only separates them from all other ventriloquists, but from all other entertainers.

Emma Taylor and Terry Fator

Finding the thing that makes them different and unique stuck with me as we filmed and I edited. But that notion really congealed after I interviewed Terry Fator. His interview is on *I'm No Dummy 2: The Not So Lost Footage*. I have seen countless people give up on their dream. To be a great writer, to be a great musician, whatever. The idea of decision, commitment, and finding that one thing that makes you different works in all artistic pursuits and oddly enough can be applied to everyday life.

Young Terry Fator With His Two Partners

```
┌─────────────────────────────────┐
│  Prologue / Teaser              │
└─────────────────────────────────┘
         │
┌─────────────────────────────────┐
│          What's ventriloquism?  │
└─────────────────────────────────┘
    │
┌─────────────────────────────────┐
│  Why vent?                      │
└─────────────────────────────────┘
    │
┌─────────────────────────────────┐
│          Don't move your lips.  │
└─────────────────────────────────┘
    │
┌─────────────────────────────────┐
│  There's two of us here!        │
└─────────────────────────────────┘
         │
┌─────────────────────────────────┐
│      What's SOAP got to do with it? │
└─────────────────────────────────┘
    │
┌─────────────────────────────────┐
│              Paul Winchell      │
│  It's old school?               │
└─────────────────────────────────┘
         │
┌─────────────────────────────────┐
│  Senor Wences                   │
│          It's old school?       │
└─────────────────────────────────┘
    │
┌─────────────────────────────────┐
│  It's old school?               │
│          Jimmy Nelson           │
└─────────────────────────────────┘
         │
┌─────────────────────────────────┐
│          It's old school?       │
│  Edgar Bergen                   │
└─────────────────────────────────┘
    │
┌─────────────────────────────────┐
│  Where do dummies go when they die? │
└─────────────────────────────────┘
    │
┌─────────────────────────────────┐
│          End of an era?         │
└─────────────────────────────────┘
    │
┌─────────────────────────────────┐
│  Epilogue                       │
└─────────────────────────────────┘
```

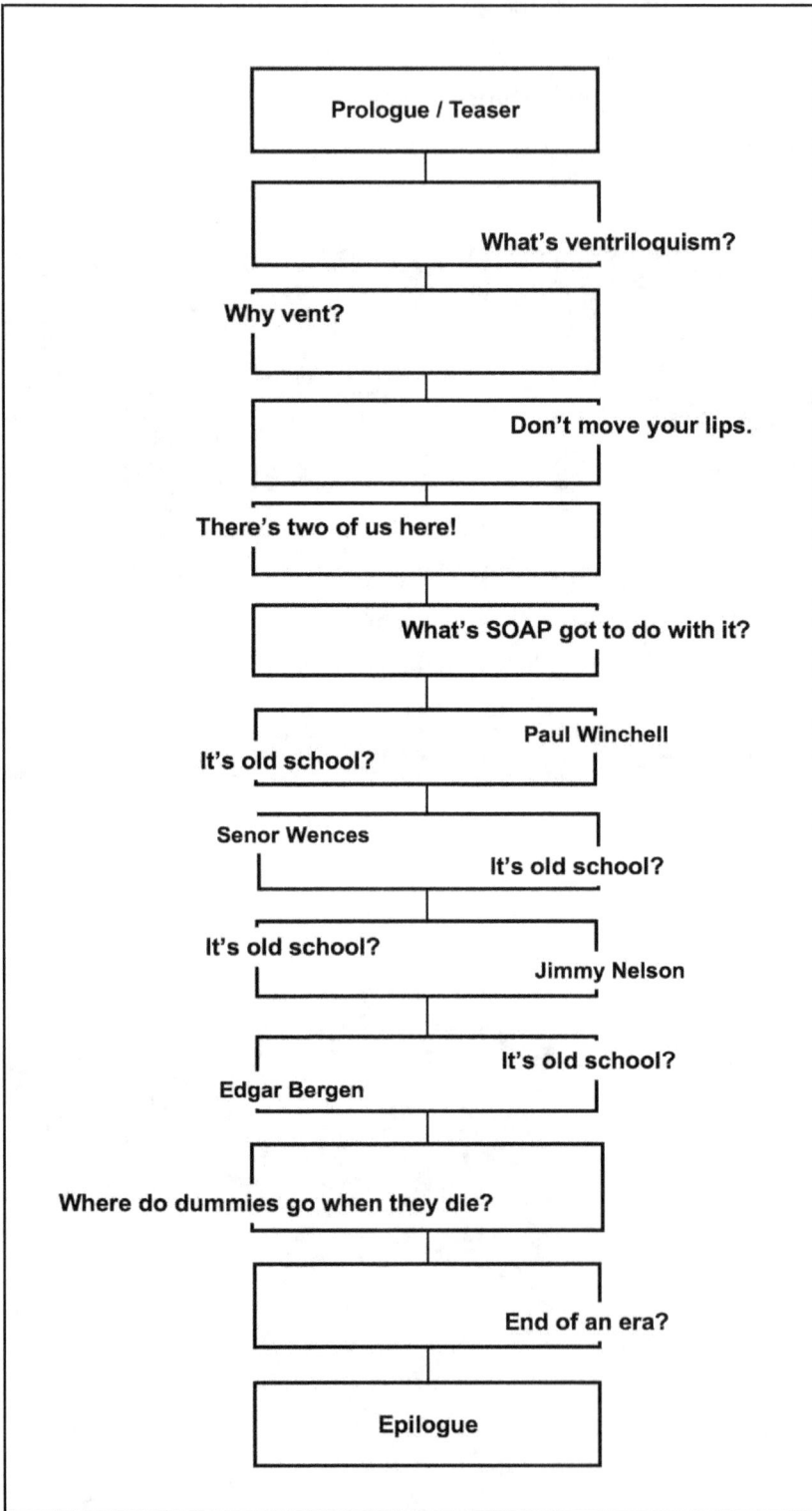

I'm No Dummy was completely plotted out and is exactly how I originally envisioned it. Even the opening puppet segment was considered in advance. There were definitely some cool surprises along the way but it's pretty much just as I saw it in my head. A lot of people say that docs are made in the editing room, and I completely disagree. No film is made in any one singular phase, because you can't edit what you haven't shot. I really stress that you have to have some plan, treatment or structure to make a good, concise and clear documentary. It's only then that you can catch some lightning that makes it special.

You need to be open to new ideas and directions, but you have to stay focused otherwise the end product will be a meandering mess. That said, I'm sure there are documentarians who have shot their docs in an improvisational way, with very little structure and made something special. But I'll bet it's rare.

Chloe and Lynn Trefzger

In my opinion, regarding films in general, the writer is the architect. As the writer, I plotted out the structure and wrote the questions. If you don't know what you're going to shoot, you're not going to have anything to cut from. I had an identical set of questions for every ventriloquist, with a few specific to each of them, and then if I thought of something during the interview I would ask that too.

I also "wrote" so to speak in the editing phase. A director is really like the conductor of a orchestra, bringing his or her vision to the project and creating space where the actors or in this case the interviewees can feel comfortable, focused and give their best performance.

Peanut and Jeff Dunham

Danny O'Day and Jimmy Nelson

The director also works with the department heads to bring their best work to the project. And finally, I believe the editor is the sculptor. Kinda like working in clay. Carving away chunks, but also adding pieces back in as the film takes shape.

Jay Johnson

We shot over 150 hours of interviews and performance footage. 54 individuals were interviewed with 19 actually appearing in the film. Some were great interviews and some weren't. You can see some of my selections of outtake footage in the extras section on the DVD and in *I'm No Dummy 2: The Not So Lost Footage* on Amazon. Filmmaking is one third planning, one third shooting, and one third post production.

Everything I've ever done, from scripted narrative to documentary to TV or a big screen adaptation of a Tony Award® winning Broadway show, was all hinged on the planning stage.

L to R: Vonda Kay Van Dyke, Kurly Q, Lloyd Freidus, and Bryan W. Simon

Below is a photo of Otto Petersen. Otto died in 2014 at the age of 53. I find his story fascinating. He started out as a street performer in Manhattan who developed an act that was raw and very adult. Although I didn't know him very well, what I do know is that he was one of the nicest people on the planet. He never really associated with other ventriloquists and was a very shy individual and didn't want to be interviewed at first. He was one of those people that you say to yourself, "I wish I had known him better and spent more time with him."

As a street performer or busker as it's called, Petersen grew up performing in Manhattan and on the Staten Island Ferry from age 13 to 21. He would often skip school to perform his art.

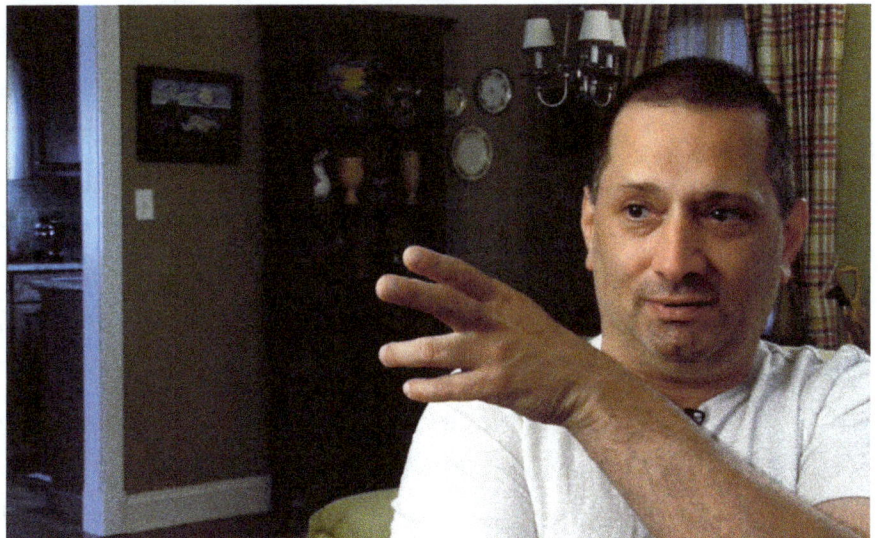

Otto Petersen

The structure of *I'm No Dummy* was adapted from a documentary I really love entitled *The Corporation* (2003). It was divided into sections or chapters and I envisioned *I'm No Dummy* similarly.

Basically it's a film that unfolds like a book in many ways, sections or chapters. I use these words interchangeably because this is like a book, and a little like a screenplay in my mind with its acts. I wanted to use the best of both structures, build on them in an ascending order. A loose screenplay act structure with a resolution and future projection at the end, keeping in mind the themes and the questions posed throughout the piece. The idea was to have a chapter or section build on the one before it. It was really the only structure I could come up with that fit what I was trying to achieve, a respectful documentary about this art form. Nearly every short doc or television segment about ventriloquists made fun of them or portrayed them as creepy. That wasn't interesting to me, because that's the easy way in my opinion.

When I first started researching and reaching out to the vent community, I was actually rebuffed. No one wanted to talk to us. They had been lied to, tricked so many times that they were very weary of filmmakers that came along and said they wouldn't make fun of them and their art, and then would do the opposite. When I reached out to Annie Roberts of Vent Haven Museum, she wouldn't speak with me initially but suggested that I contact Kelly Asbury, a feature animation director from Hollywood. He had written a book about the golden age of ventriloquism, entitled *Dummy Days*. I called Kelly at his Disney Studio office and asked him if we could get together for an on-camera interview. He said yes, but it would have to be right away because he was headed to London to direct, so we picked a date and we filmed an interview with him at his home.

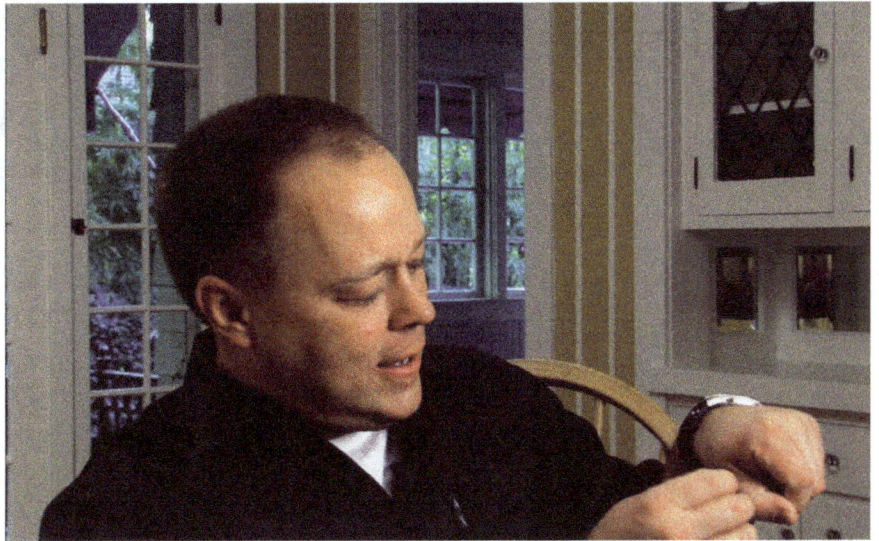

Kelly Asbury

It really was Kelly who vouched for us to the vent community. He contacted several people and let them know I was a competent director and my intentions were to discuss this much-maligned art form in a serious and respectful way. After that, everything pretty much fell into place. Word spread and we were able to contact people and set up interviews.

Once we defined ventriloquism in the artist's own words and learned why they do what they do, I felt we should tackle one of the most important parts of ventriloquism, lip control. Without some lip control, you're just a puppeteer, which is great, but that doesn't make you a ventriloquist. There is a prevalent misconception that puppeteer Wayland Flowers was a ventriloquist. He had a figure, Madam, that he used on countless TV and stage shows and he was NOT A VENTRILOQUIST. He himself would have to constantly correct people and tell them he was a puppeteer.

Waylon Flowers and Madame

27

There's two of us here!

I've been asked what my favorite section is in this film and that's like asking which one of your children you like the best. I love every one of my films and every part of each film. I don't regret or rethink stuff. It's a waste of time. It is what it is, at the time I made it. That it isn't to say I wouldn't do some things differently now. That's improving your art or craft.

Simon and Lynn Trefzger

If you put a gun to my head and say pick your favorite section, I'd say it's this one: "There's Two of Us Here!" not because I think it's better than any of the others, but because I think it surprised me the most of any of the sections. When you're making a film, you have certain expectations and as I have said you need to be open to surprises within your structure or idea. This was the only section that evolved from one idea into a larger idea. The initial thought started out as a question just about that comedy bit of having the puppet call out the ventriloquist for their lip control or making a mistake, and ended up being a discussion on something much deeper; revealing the trick and why that is so psychologically important.

Camelot and Lynn Trefzger

"There's Two of Us Here!" is really about revealing the trick to the audience so that the illusion works even better.

Jay Johnson explains this so well:

[Jay Johnson] "...but the genius of that is that you never want the audience to forget how hard you're working at that. The tendency is that if you're so good they suddenly think of you as two people and then you're judged on what two people can or can't do. You must continually remind them that this is me doing this, I have fooled you and this brings you back to that "oh my, I'm back to reality, oh, oh" then you break that reality again and then it's, "oh that's right, he's just doing that," and that becomes your comedy arc, that's becomes your way to get back to it, that's the way to remind the audience that this is ventriloquism and that it's not two stand ups. This is reminding them that they've been fooled."

Bob and Jay Johnson

Charlie Brown and Arthur Worsley

Ventriloquist Arthur Worsley is one of my favorite vents. His act is truly surreal. I am just so intrigued by his ability to communicate without saying a word. To have a conversation without speaking. By the way, what he is actually saying is "gottle o' geer." He's using a form of letter substitution to make it sound as if Charlie Brown is saying bottle of beer. We'll talk about that technique in Jimmy Nelson's section.

I want to talk a little bit about this clip of Jimmy and Danny doing their smoking routine. The song they sing together is entitled "The Best Things in Life Are Free." When we interviewed Jimmy about this extremely popular routine that they did, he stated on camera that he wanted to be very clear that he stopped doing that routine when the health hazards of smoking became obvious, and that he and his wife Betty eventually became spokespersons and advocates for the American Lung Association. So why do I mention this? Because when you make a documentary you almost always have to edit these asides and comments out, for continuity of thought and flow of the piece and I felt bad about doing that. No doubt he was worried that people might think that he still does that routine, which he felt was inappropriate. This short segment of clips and interview with Jimmy perfectly illustrates how fair use is applied and how it can be an artistic asset.

Danny O'Day and Jimmy Nelson

When Lisa Callif viewed the whole film, she had some notes about our fair use practice and this clip was one of them. In my original cut it was not divided up, the two pieces were together and it was even a little longer. She felt that it was too long and asked me to cut down that clip. So I came up with the idea to cut the routine in two and intercut Jimmy's interview to divide it all up. I actually think this segment works even better than originally planned and that was because Lisa demanded that I think more deeply about it in order to satisfy the fair use doctrine.

Walter and Jeff Dunham

[Tom Ladshaw] *"There is not only the suspension of disbelief, but the suspension of belief there on the puppets part."*

Tom Ladshaw

[Jay Johnson] *"Always remind them that you're doing it. It's funny, but it's so... It has such depth of reality."*

Jay Johnson

In regards to television, there was a phrase that was used for a while, where the next morning after an episode aired, people stood around the water cooler at work and talked about what had happened, how funny or shocking it had been. The term for that type of television show was "water cooler show."

OPEN CALL FOR VENTRILOQUIST

20 to 30 years old
Available for TV series

CBS-TV City
Fairfax & Beverly
Rehearsal Hall Room B-2

Monday, August 8
10 a.m. to 12 noon

This section is very personal to me and is important because of its modern historical context. Like most everyone, I found out about Jay Johnson when he was cast on *SOAP*. *SOAP* is credited as being the very first "water cooler show". If you hadn't seen the previous nights episode, you felt left out as your co-workers chatted about it. Because of *SOAP*, I went to see Jay in the comedy clubs in Chicago. *SOAP* really rocketed Jay to fame and he opened up the comedy club circuit for the vents that followed. Before him, ventriloquists were not welcomed in comedy clubs. It was this show, and Jay Johnson, that brought ventriloquism from the golden era into the modern age. Every time Jay was in Chicago, my friends and I would take the train into the city and see him in the club. When he was working on his Broadway show, *Jay Johnson: The Two & Only!*, Marge and I went to see an early version at the Brentwood Theater in Los Angeles. This was about eight months before that bike ride where I thought of doing the documentary. I've been asked the question many times if Jay's show was some trigger for the idea. Seeing it certainly didn't hurt and kept that art form in my mind, but it wasn't an "aha" moment.

Since the first interview for *I'm No Dummy*, Jay and I have become good friends and collaborators. He's one of the nicest, most supportive, and smartest guys I know. It's crazy how his mind works, he's a real artist.

Bob and Jay Johnson

SOAP originally ran on ABC from 1977 through 1981. The show was created as a nighttime parody of daytime soap operas presented as a weekly half-hour prime time comedy. It was included in *Time* magazine's "100 Best TV Shows of All Time," and ranked number 17 in *TV Guide*'s list of "TV's Top Families". *SOAP* often swept its time slot with as much as a 26 rating and 39 percent share. A 39% share means of everyone watching TV, over one third were watching *SOAP*. That's an unheard of number today. ABC received hundreds of phone calls after the premiere. The show was pretty controversial. A poll found that 26% found it offensive. What's funny about that is, half of those were still going to watch it the next week.

Jay Sandrich, Bob, and Jay Johnson

Publicity Photos from SOAP, 1977-1981

[Jay Johnson] *"They were really clueless about what ventriloquism was until I got involved and I was able to tailor what needed to be done a lot of times. I suggested a lot of things I got to do on the show simply because I knew that my survival on the show was dependent on how many different ways I could be used on that show. Because I had seen characters written in and then written out, written in, written out. I was supposed to be there for seven shows and stayed for four years."*

At the end of the *SOAP* section, *I'm No Dummy* touches briefly on Jay's Tony Award® winning Broadway show. I didn't realize at the time it was foreshadowing a new collaboration with Jay. In 2012, Jay, Sandi – Jay's wife, Marge and I talked about the possibility of preserving the show. In my opinion, not done enough with Broadway shows. Marge and I thought with our background in theater, having run a professional theater company in the Chicago area, and now with our filmmaking abilities, we were a great fit. In late 2012, I directed and Marge produced the big screen adaptation of *Jay Johnson: The Two & Only!* at the historic Thalian Hall in Wilmington, North Carolina. A trailer is on the front end of the *I'm No Dummy* DVD and a short segment from the show is on the second disc of extras.

Squeaky and Jay Johnson from Jay Johnson: The Two & Only!

It was in 2007 that Jay won the Tony Award® for his ventriloquial Broadway show. It ranks as one of the greatest milestones in vent history. Jay Johnson's "partner" Bob has a second home in the Smithsonian Institution's National Museum of American History in Washington D.C.

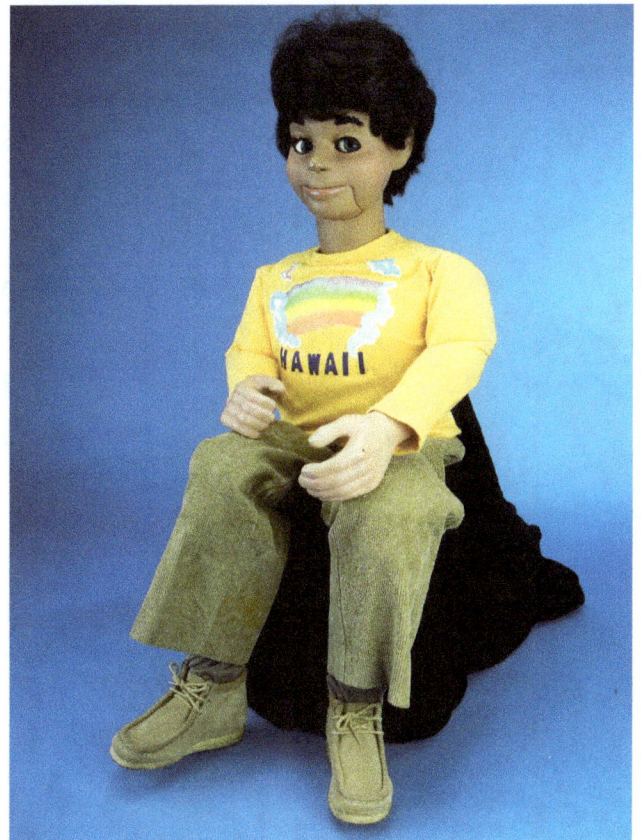

Bob at the Smithsonian

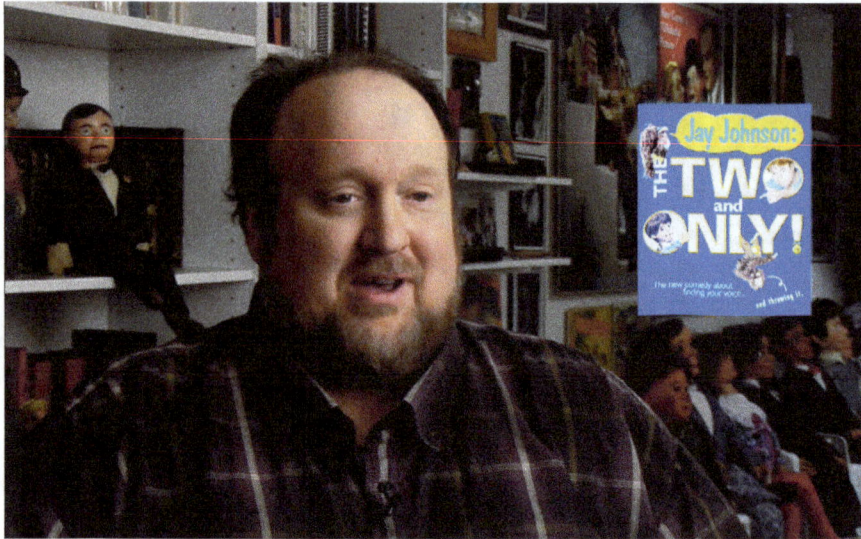

Tom Ladshaw

[Tom Ladshaw] *"With Jay's one man show on Broadway and I can tell you, Jay knocked 'em dead and got a standing ovation, and again that's one more way that Jay Johnson is doing his part and ventriloquism's profile is getting raised again."*

Tom Ladshaw wraps up this section and I can not overstate his contribution to the film. He is a very talented ventriloquist and magician as well as one of the most knowledgeable authorities on the history of ventriloquism. He guided me, but yet always allowed me to make the documentary I wanted to make. He was given the designation of Associate Producer because of his tireless work on our behalf.

It's old school?

"It's Old School," with its four historical figures, was in many ways the most difficult section to construct. Paul Winchell, Señor Wences, Jimmy Nelson, and Edgar Bergen could easily have their own documentaries.

Kelly Asbury told me he was happy I was doing this documentary. He wanted to do a documentary film version of his book *Dummy Days*, but knew that he would never get to it. In some small way this section is inspired by *Dummy Days*.

Headlined by Paul Winchell, Señor Wences, Jimmy Nelson, and Edgar Bergen, the following includes information more about the making of the film rather than about the ventriloquists themselves.

PAUL WINCHELL

Because I didn't want the historical figures' sections to become unwieldy, I decided to concentrate on just one aspect of their careers which in my opinion significantly changed ventriloquism. After viewing their sections, if people want to learn more about these particular vents there is a lot of information out there about their careers and lives.

Great artists learn and grow from other great artists, and in the modern world of ventriloquism this is still the case. In many ways, the great ventriloquists currently working today have also changed the art form.

Jerry Mahoney and Paul Winchell

As we interviewed participants, they would make suggestions about someone else that might be an interesting subject. We never paid anyone for an interview. Even though some of the vents were members of the Screen Actors Guild, the union rules don't apply to documentaries and payment is not necessary. We did run into some strange requests and responses though.

As mentioned before, I was warned you can't make friends with subjects, a theory I don't necessarily espouse. I was also cautioned that a potential subject might dictate how, when, or even the direction of my interview. This happened at least three times. I would not interview anyone if there were too many barriers or requirements.

Ed Sullivan, Jerry Mahoney, and Paul Winchell

There was a former ventriloquist I contacted early on who I never met. Every conversation was over the phone or by Email. He fancied himself an expert on one of our old school vents, having worked with that vent in the past, and he wanted to be paid. I told him he couldn't get paid, no one is. He said he was in the actors union and so he had to get paid. I told him I had already checked, and no, you don't have to get paid. I was not going to pay him. We never spoke again.

There was another expert on the east coast who we wanted to interview for his knowledge of one of the old school vents.

Jerry Mahoney and Paul Winchell

A couple days before we flew out, he called me and said he couldn't do the interview because he was rearranging his collection and he wanted his collection in the background when we filmed him. I told him I wasn't sure where I was going to film him until we were there, and, to be honest, it's the interview that's important, not his collection. We were doing a lot of interviews on the east coast and scheduling was difficult. He said we'd have to

do it some other time. A month later he contacted me and said, "I'm ready." I explained that I got plenty of information from other experts who were available when we filmed earlier, and we wouldn't be interviewing him.

Then there was one collector that wanted the footage immediately. There was no way I could provide footage right after shooting. I told him I'd be happy to share it later when filming was done, but that didn't satisfy him. So we never interviewed him.

Early on, I did worry about what might be missed from the unscheduled interviews. The truth is no one is indispensable in a documentary like this. This film came out better than I ever could have imagined so perhaps none of those people were needed.

Jerry Mahoney and Paul Winchell

Paul Winchell's Gypsy song is crazy good. The choreography is really amazing and he is a terrific actor. I don't have one favorite ventriloquist. The documentary taught me that every ventriloquist we featured contributed to the art form in a way that cannot be underestimated.

Jerry Mahoney and Paul Winchell

I had to figure out what order the four ventriloquists would go in this section, so the criteria was a combination of contribution, structure and overall timing in the film.

Paul Winchell, like all great ventriloquists, built on what the best vents of the past had done. He took an older style of ventriloquism, the scene or short play, and made it his own. Winchell animated the figure in a way no one had ever done. He influenced a lot of modern ventriloquists, but interestingly, no one has really been able to duplicate his amazing ability to bring that puppet off the knee. He had a TV show where he used an assistant, Jay Lloyd, to work the puppet's body, arms, and hands while Winchell worked the head and voice. It takes a lot of rehearsal with these complicated scenes to do this. Today all of the working vents are on a live stage. No one is doing a ventriloquist TV show like Paul Winchell did.

I love the length of this film. I wouldn't go back and recut a thing. No extended director's cut. When plotting it, I made a conscious effort to figure out how long each segment or chapter would be and how long the entire film would be. I knew there had to be a funny clip every minute or two. And I didn't want too many talking heads. There's a screenwriting adage; if you are writing a comedy film, you better try to have a huge laugh on every page. Makes sense to me.

Quite a few ventriloquists felt that *I'm No Dummy* could have been longer but I didn't make this documentary for ventriloquists; I made it for people like me. A lot more material and subjects could have been covered. I resisted loading up the doc because I wanted it to be a manageable length for watching. My goal was to entertain and illuminate the general public about this art form. I also wanted to "leave them wanting more." Which is something Jeff Dunham mentions early on in the film. I didn't want anyone to be bored.

We had to be as economical as possible in shooting *I'm No Dummy*, because of our very limited budget. I came up with the idea of buying a good used camera and then gambling that we could resell it. With our Director of Photography Lloyd Freidus' help, we ended up finding a used Sony Z1U professional camcorder, which shot high definition 1080i pictures, used Mini DV tapes, not cards, and also had two-channel recording. Everything we needed for the documentary. Technology moves at a witheringly fast pace these days, and not long after we bought this camera, it became obsolete.

Jerry Mahoney and Paul Winchell

So what does that mean? It meant I could shoot an HD documentary for very little. We purchased the used Z1U from Roger Corman's company, which was kinda cool in and of itself, and they tossed in a couple of extras for two thousand dollars. It took almost a year to shoot the film, so it would have cost much more to rent a decent camera every time we went out, on average every other week for two to three days. When we were done, we sold the camera for that same amount we had purchased it for. Lloyd brought along a few pieces of his lighting equipment and sound gear, which meant we could travel light. It was just Lloyd, my wife Marge, and myself.

On a few occasions when we needed a second camera to film performances, Christopher Gray from Gray Post Production in Santa Monica loaned us another Z1U.

41

SEÑOR WENCES

I'm No Dummy was cut in sections, not in the order that comprises the finished film. The Senor Wences section was the first one I cut and screened. It was also the section that was locked after the first cut.

By the way, *I'm No Dummy* is the second film Lloyd and I made together. He shot my very first film in 1995, entitled *The Second Room*.

Norm Nielsen

Norm Nielsen was Señor Wences good friend. Norm is a retired magician and we interviewed him at his home in Las Vegas. Internationally known, Norm performed all over the world, and met Señor Wences when the two of them appeared at the world famous Crazy Horse Saloon in Paris. He and Wences were there for many years. Initially Norm was hesitant to appear on camera. He's actually very shy, but we convinced him to see us and he ended up being a really terrific addition to the Wences section. As a magician, Norm's signature trick was the floating violin. The violin floats in the air and the bow floats as well, moving across the strings playing the violin. No one knows how this was done and he never revealed the secret. It took him several years to perfect that extremely intricate illusion. Sadly, Norm passed in 2020.

There is a pattern in how I framed the interviews. The ventriloquists are always on camera right, your right side, and all non ventriloquists were on camera left. I wanted to keep these people separate visually and it made sense to have the ventriloquist on the right side of the frame so that I wouldn't have to flip the vent when the puppet was appearing with them.

When performing, the primary puppet is always on the right. But when someone like Jimmy Nelson is working with two puppets, then the second puppet is on the left side. I also wanted to do something I called "picture-in-picture" framing. Instead of cutting away from the person being interviewed, to help illustrate their point, I put an additional picture in that negative space that is to their right or left.

Theo and Stevo Schüling

Tom Ladshaw

There were times I didn't use picture-in-picture. Why was that? Two reasons: one, I wanted to give greater importance to that little picture by making it full frame so we would focus only on that image, and secondly, to mask a cut. The person being interviewed may have gone on a tangent, or maybe something on the front end of the answer worked great with something on the back end. And I had to cut out the middle of the answer. If I had something to cut to, I could fill the frame and cover up the cut. I'm not a big fan of using a jump cut in interviews. The jump cut is when you cut to the dialogue making all of that smooth, but what we see is the person hopping or moving slightly on the screen, in a very unnatural way. There is just one spot where I was forced to do that toward the end of the film.

Ed Sullivan, Señor Wences, and Johnny

Once I knew what my framing would be, I had to decide the "mise en scene." Mise en scène refers to everything that appears before the camera and that arrangement: like the composition, sets, props, actors, costumes, and lighting. Seems simple enough but there are many documentarians that have everyone sit in front of a green screen and then put in some sort of color or background.

Then there are others who put everyone in front of a blank wall and throw a little light behind them. This definitely focuses our attention on the subject, but I wanted to have a lot more going on, and a more natural, less synthetic background while discussing this very surreal subject of speaking to oneself.

Lloyd and I worked together to find the best place to set up an interview. Kelly Asbury's house was completely empty, as he was getting ready to rent it before his move to London. We chose the dining room. For Burt Dubrow, Paul Winchell's friend, we found a spot with good light with his collection of figures in the background. If you look closely you can see the look-a-like-puppet of Paul Winchell that is featured in a clip we used. In Jay's home, you can see a Broadway show poster behind him. When we interviewed people at the ventriloquist convention, we had to rearrange and dress a hotel room. It was really the only place quiet enough to do

Burt Dubrow

interviews. We threw the bed up against the wall, ran to Walmart down the street, got a fake plant or two and borrowed a few books from Tom Ladshaw to place on the desk. I think it looks pretty good.

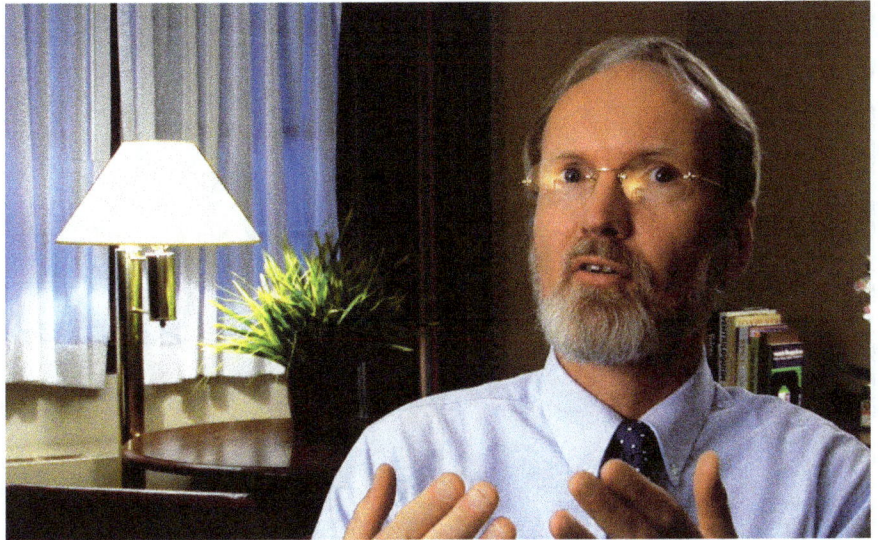

Stevo Schüling

Cameras, lights and all of those things are just tools. You can have a really expensive hammer or a really cheap one, but they both pound nails. Obviously expensive equipment is more likely to last longer, but with film technology changing constantly, that expensive camera will be obsolete sooner than later. The most important thing to remember in filmmaking is that film equipment doesn't make films, filmmakers make films. It starts in your imagination and then you figure out how to make it. It's about art and imagination, not the coolest equipment. Below is an outtake piece of our interview with Jay Johnson about imagination.

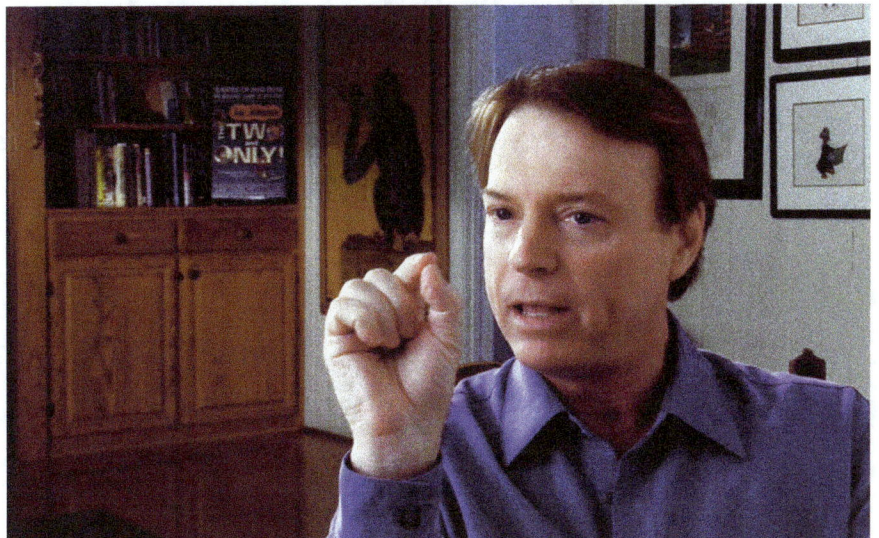

Jay Johnson

[Jay Johnson] *"Imagination, yeah, there's no more powerful word in the world. Because we see things in the world of imagination, we are not bound by the codes and the numbers or the structure of the alphabet. We can spell anything the way we want to. There's a rule to spell it this way, but in our imagination that word is spelled just as good as anything. And in our imagination, two and two doesn't have to be four, two and two can be anything you want. Works out fine. With imagination you can go anywhere. Albert Einstein said, "imagination is more*

45

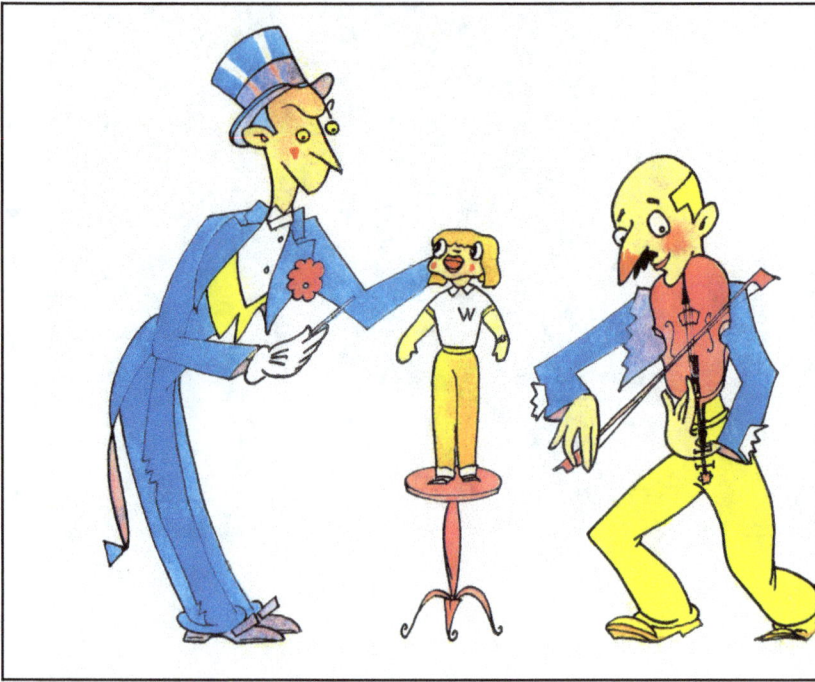

Sketch by Señor Wences

important than knowledge. And I believe that one hundred percent because imagination is how you use knowledge. If you think of knowledge as water in a pot, then imagination is the steam that is created by the fire, that lights up that knowledge. Causing it to change into a form that can run turbines. But in and of itself, knowledge is just sitting there. Water's just sitting there until it's boiled, makes steam, which runs things. Yeah, imagination. If it's not done in imagination first, it's not done."

JIMMY NELSON

Jimmy Nelson's contribution to the art of ventriloquism cannot be underestimated. He is in my opinion the greatest influence in the era of television, inspiring a new generation of ventriloquists in a way that no one else had.

Kelly Asbury

[Kelly Asbury] *"They had Jimmy Nelson's instructional album, so many people working today go back to that."*

[Jeff Dunham] *"Jimmy Nelson's album was the perfect teacher for me, both of them, Instant Ventriloquism and the follow up, the blue one. I think it was great because he hit upon a very simple way of teaching and learning ventriloquism that anybody could follow and understand."*

I think Jimmy's section has special meaning for me, because Marge and I became very good friends with Jimmy and his wife Betty. Jimmy and Betty were two of the most wonderful people you could meet. Marge and I created and maintain Jimmy's personal website, *jimmydannyfarfel.com* where you can find out so much more about Jimmy's amazing

Danny O'Day, Jimmy Nelson, and Farfel

career as well as Betty's work in entertainment. If you have a few minutes, check it out. There's also an illustrated book about Jimmy's career entitled, *A Jimmy Nelson Celebration: 70 Years of Laughter*, written by Tom Ladshaw. Sadly, Jimmy Nelson passed away on September 24, 2019 at age 90.

[Tom Ladshaw] *"On the original Jimmy Nelson album he espouses the philosophy of sound substitution using for instance the letter D for B. And what Jimmy always says and says to this day…"*

[Jimmy Nelson] *"You say D, but you think B. So it doesn't come out D, but it comes out B. So it's a softer sound and it sounds much more like a B than a D."*

[Tom Ladshaw] *"So instead of saying Basketball, you say Dasketdoll and you think Basketball. So with the lips in the proper position and the teeth in the proper position and the tongue in the proper position, so instead of it sounding like Dasketdoll, it should sound like Basketball."*

At *I'm No Dummy* screenings in Seattle, New York City and Los Angeles, when Tom says, "Basketball" ventriloquially, there was always an audible response from the audience. They would uniformly go "ooohhh." It was amazing. I think when it's broken down so clearly and effectively, it really sinks in how the letters are formed by ventriloquists. I got a kick out of that universal response.

Stevo Schüling on Editing Screens

This was the first film I ever edited. I don't like editing my own work. I was my last choice to edit it but I lost two editors because of the shear volume of the footage and the time constraints. I wanted to have it finished as fast as possible so it was out of necessity that I took on the task. Editing is redirecting in many ways, and I believe there should be another set of eyes and skills, to bring out the best in a feature film.

Unlike a scripted narrative film, feature documentaries are handled a little differently. I relied on a few friends that are directors, producers, and editors to give me notes along the way. There wasn't a lot of notes, but Ed Salier who cut my very first film, and has been an editorial consultant on every one of my films since, was my major second set of eyes and had the skills I needed.

His notes were invaluable and I really appreciated his input. He helped me with a big decision about something that needed to be cut out which I'll talk about later.

Before we even shot one frame, we met with Michael Cioni and Paul Geffre of Light Iron Post Production. At the time, they were both at the now defunct Plaster City in Hollywood. I was cutting in Final Cut Pro and I wanted to understand what my workflow would be. I didn't want to screw things up when shooting and then try to fix it later in post. When you don't have a lot of money, that's not an option. I thought it was a good idea to talk about the editing process first so that I could make sure that we were shooting and prepping things in the right way.

How would we frame the archival footage is one of the many things that I learned and decided at that meeting with Michael and Paul.

You have this great old clip you want to use, but it's not the same size frame that you're shooting or will finally project on screen. All of the archival footage we needed came in at 4 by 3 not 16 by 9. This means the width by the height of the frame, image or screen. The size of the old standard television or film clip was 4:3 or 4 by 3 ratio or 1.33. Television screens started out the size of the frame of film and all archival footage tends to be that way. TV screens are now 16 by 9, or a compromise between the old TV screen and a wide screen movie theater image. So my dilemma was: do I leave my archival footage 4 by 3 and put black pillars, as they are called, on each side? Or, do I blow up that 4 by 3 image, making it bigger to fit the 16 by 9 frame we were shooting in by cropping out some of the top and bottom of that original frame?

You follow me?

Michael and Paul showed us a doc that kept the archival footage it's normal frame size with the pillars. But to me it was jarring to go from a 16 x 9 image to a 4 by 3 image, and then back again to

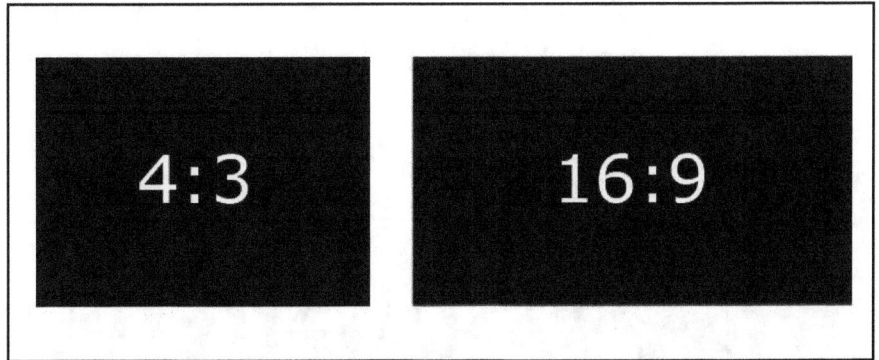

Top: 4x3 Original Framing with Black Pillars
Bottom: 16x9 Conversion

the 16 x 9. I decided right then to blow up the old footage and make it all flow together seamlessly. I didn't want to take the viewer out of the moment and make the archival footage, which was typically black and white and grainy, more obvious than it already was. And every time there is a cut in a film to a new place or angle or person, it takes a second or two for the viewers mind to orient itself. I felt the cut would be even more jarring if the images didn't match in size.

Danny O'Day, Jimmy Nelson, and Farfel

We took the same approach for touching up and fixing photos. Some of the old photos we acquired from collectors and the museum were messed up, and if we used any of those photos, Marge would touch them up in Photoshop. She is really skilled at that. Again, I wanted the transition to be as seamless as possible. I remember seeing a documentary where they didn't fix the old pictures that had been really damaged over time. Subconsciously I said to myself, "wow that's a messed up picture," so it took me a moment to get back on track in the film. If the photo wasn't messed up, I'd see it, appreciate it, and move on with the story. If we have the technology to get photographs back to what they once were, or as close as possible, why not?

I never get tired of watching Jimmy and Danny's rendition of "Ragg Mop." Part of Jimmy's legacy is that he was a friend to everyone. Especially in the vent community. Jimmy and Betty helped make the world a better place, one person at a time.

Danny O'Day, Jimmy Nelson, and Humphrey Higsby

EDGAR BERGEN

One question I asked all of the vents was, "How much do you improvise and how much is set? Walk us through that part of the stage show process." I learned that there is very little improvisation. It may not look that way, but there's almost none. After we had filmed much of the documentary, I heard Jeff speak at the ventriloquist convention about building your act, and I thought it was interesting that he will try out a few new bits or jokes at almost every concert. They're buried in the set, so if the bits or jokes don't quite work, no one notices. And if after a few tries, they don't get the right response, they're discarded or reworked; if they're working, he'll often add them to the show.

When filming Jeff in Cleveland, Tom Ladshaw and Lisa Sweasy from Vent Haven Museum met us there to see the show and hang out. We all

Achmed and Jeff Dunham

sat together in the back of the auditorium as Lloyd and our second camera operator, Eric Stewart, filmed. During the act, Jeff improvised a line for Walter that really got a huge laugh. Without missing a beat he said, "I gotta write that down." Lisa turned to me and said "That's my cue to remember it for him." He knew all of us were in the audience and just in case he forgot it later, Lisa would remember. Very clever way of making sure something spontaneous survived, and also, it revealed the trick to the audience.

As mentioned previously, we interviewed 54 people and 19 appear in the film. What's interesting about interviewing people is that everyone has their own way of speaking, telling a story, or answering a question. Some are very succinct, some ramble on, some try to be too funny, some go off on tangents, some don't finish their sentences before starting their next thought, and a few were just plain terrible interviews. That doesn't mean they aren't in the film. It means the footage is harder to edit.

Bryan W. Simon and Lloyd Freidus

The director/subject relationship is really tricky. You have to make your interviewees comfortable, have them trust you, but yet, you have to be prepared to kick them off the bus. I believe you have to serve the piece. You have to respect what you are doing so much that, on occasion, you must put your personal feelings aside and cut something out that you absolutely love.

One interview was very disappointing. The participant was a psychiatrist, and I had such high hopes for the outcome, because when we did a pre-interview on the phone, he was really great. And then when we got to his house, he was terrible. I remember it so well, he wouldn't commit to anything that we spoke about on the phone. He danced around the questions, was tentative with his answers and it was a useless trip. I felt bad for him, but what can you do. In my opinion, it didn't make a difference. You learn in making a film like this that nothing, and I mean nothing, hinges on any one thing or interview.

Edgar Bergen in the skit "The Operation"

Fortunately, I liked and respected everyone I interviewed, so it was easy to interact with them. But some subjects had unrealistic expectations. 54 minus 19 leaves 35 people that didn't make it into the film. I called everyone who didn't make the final cut because I felt I owed it to them.

As I mentioned earlier, Ed Salier helped me with a difficult editing decision. Even though I had my chapter structure, I thought that I would weave the young, talented ventriloquist Bryan Gerber in with the pros. We shot him at his home, performing at the ConVENTion, and then back home again. Something didn't feel right, so I had Ed view my first cut. He gave me a great piece of advice. He told me, this kid's really good but he will be compared to the best of the best, and that doesn't help the film. I decided to cut Bryan Gerber out completely and two things happened that I never expected.

First, Ed was stunned I actually cut this really nice kid out and said it was a gutsy move. But as I've stated, you have to serve the piece. And second, Bryan himself could not have been more gracious or understanding when we told him he would not be in the film when it came out. Bryan is now a fine ventriloquist and wonderful magician, following in his late father Paul's footsteps.

Lester and Willie Tyler

A story that Willie Tyler told me off camera was the catalyst for my calling everyone. Willie performed in a film and invited all of his friends to the film premiere. He wasn't in it. No one had let him know he had been cut. Willie was so embarrassed. From then on any movie he was in, he would go to see by himself before he told anyone else about it.

When I made the phone calls, I got varying responses from people who didn't make it into the documentary. And I was a little surprised. There were several people that said "I didn't expect to be in it, if you cut me out, I'm OK with that." "If you need the room just cut me out." That was kind of refreshing. There were a few that of course were disappointed, I'd expect that, but they were very gracious. And then there was one, a ventriloquist, that acted like a four-year-old who was told he couldn't get ice cream. If it wasn't so sad, it would have been hysterical. He said things like "You said I was so good after my interview, so why am I not in the documentary?" I really believe that some people thought that if they got into *I'm No Dummy*, it would change their lives in some way.

Jay Johnson opened the door for us when it came to distribution. Obviously you have to have a good film, but someone making introductions really helps. It's often about connections and connecting the dots. Salient Media was an independent entertainment company that created and distributed comedy content. Their cofounder, Gary Binkow, and Head of Production, Niloo Badie, approached Jay about producing a DVD version of his Broadway show *Jay Johnson: The Two & Only!*. They wanted to change the show into more of a stand up act as opposed to the theatrical event it was and Jay passed. But he did suggest to them that they consider *I'm No Dummy*. They took a look at a DVD screener and we had a meeting. Gary, believe it or not, had a Danny O'Day Juro

puppet when he was a kid, so he got it right away. He then showed it to his kids who really enjoyed it as well.

We agreed in principal right then and there and within a month the distribution deal was pounded out. It was for five years with some incentives for Salient to push hard. They did push hard getting NBC/Universal involved.

In those initial discussions with Gary and Niloo, I explained that I did not want a large and expensive theatrical release. All of that expense would come out of our profits, not theirs. It's really about crunching the numbers. Vanity aside, they just weren't there. As time goes on I'm less and less a fan of film festivals in general, only a couple can actually help your film, and even then it's pretty hit and miss. We agreed that we would not spend much on festivals.

Bryan W. Simon and Marjorie Engesser

However we were in a couple film festivals in 2009 before Salient released *I'm No Dummy* on DVD in 2010. Thomas Ethan Harris came on board as our film festival consultant, something he no longer does, since he has transitioned into producing. He helped us get into the Seattle International Film Festival, a festival that's highly regarded internationally and well attended. Even with an advocate like Thomas, it wasn't easy to get into the festival. One of the hurdles was the fact that festivals don't think much of comedic films, and even less of comedic docs.

While we were attending the first screening in Seattle, a gentleman came up to me and said that he was on the documentary programming committee for the festival. He informed us *I'm No Dummy* kept being pushed aside. When it came up for one of the last slots, he stood up in the meeting and said "Can we please program a terrific documentary that's very funny? We keep programming homeless children docs and this one is really different and special." Now documentaries about homeless children are

Early Charlie and Edgar Bergen

really important, every doc is important in it's own way, but what he was saying was audiences need to get a variety and comedy isn't a bad thing. I couldn't thank him enough.

No matter what type of film you make, festivals are a beast. If you just want a few people to see your film, great, then I would suggest entering every festival you can, but if you want a festival to be a jumping off platform for a big release, don't plan on it.

Because of it's popularity, *I'm No Dummy* got three screenings in Seattle, not the traditional two and was sold out every time. It was hugely popular and ended up getting another two screenings later that year in Seattle. The Q and A's were really fun, the best ones that I've ever had for any of my films at a festival. Tom Ladshaw, Jay Johnson, and Lynn Trefzger all came out with their puppets and you can see some of those Q & A's on the DVD extras and on our *I'm No Dummy* Facebook page. It was really a wonderful experience.

The other film festival we were in was the New York International Children's Film Festival. They reached out to us and we were happy to be a part of it. Again Lynn, Tom and Jay along with Marge and I attended. The ventriloquists gave a wonderful class just for this festival to everyone who attended. We produced a children's book on how to make a sock puppet, gave out a sock and markers to all kids in attendance, and instead of the usual Q & A, the vents along with their puppets gave a class. It was really fun and sold out as well.

L to R: Bryan W. Simon, Tom Ladshaw, Jay Johnson, Lynn Trefzger, and Marjorie Engesser

Reviews are a necessary evil in filmmaking. The first one came out of the Seattle International Film Festival, and now, it's much harder to get professional reviews for your work. When you send a piece of art into the world, alone and unprotected, you have to be prepared for varying responses, some good, some bad. I've been fortunate to have many wonderful reviews for my films. *I'm No Dummy* was no exception in that regard.

Bob and Jay Johnson,Chloe and Lynn Trefzger, Marjorie Engesser

Kurt Dahlke of *DVD Talk* stated, "Prepare to have your socks knocked off by *I'm No Dummy*. At an engrossing 90-minutes, the documentary makes its point with emphasis. Read my lips. HIGHLY RECOMMENDED." Patrick Hickey, Jr. from *ReviewFix.com* said, "*I'm No Dummy* is a quality piece of cinema" and "charming, thoughtful and fun from start to finish." And on Westwood One Radio, renowned critic Chuck Rich said, "I fell in love with this documentary within the opening minutes." Good reviews are helpful to sell a film, but they also indicate that reviewers understand what you are trying to share with your audience.

Dr. David Goldblatt's comments ends this sequence, and they apply to all art forms. Without the artist, there would not be any art and without the art, the artist would not exist. All forms of art are ventriloquial when you get right down to it.

Edgar Bergen and Charlie McCarthy

[Dr. David Goldblatt]   "The origin of the dummy is the ventriloquist, but in some ways the origin of the ventriloquist is also the dummy, because Edgar Bergen would not be Edgar Bergen without Charlie McCarthy."

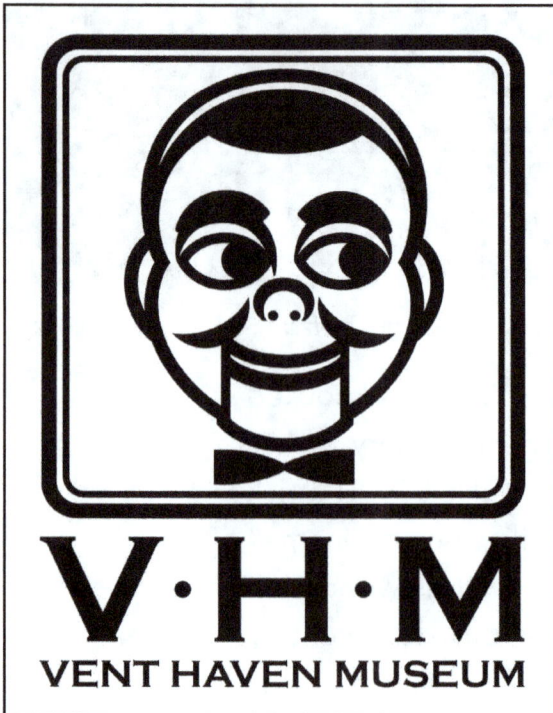

Vent Haven Museum Logo

When we were chatting about the rough cut, a good friend from my hometown of Waukegan, Illinois, Christopher Alvarado, a very talented composer and musician who has scored a few things for me, joked that the museum "is where puppets go to die." I knew then and there that was the title for this section about Vent Haven Museum, the only museum in the world dedicated to the art of ventriloquism. There is so much I could have put in about the museum. I'm really grateful that our distributor Doug Zwick encouraged us to release *I'm No Dummy 2: The Not So Lost Footage*. It has some terrific segments about the museum that I just couldn't fit in the documentary. I wanted to give the audience a brief overview of this art form and the museum in the documentary. And hopefully they would want to see more and perhaps visit Vent Haven when they were in the Cincinnati area.

Vent Haven Museum Entrance Sign

Museum Curator Lisa Sweasy, Historian Tom Ladshaw, and Museum Board Member Annie Roberts were absolutely invaluable. They provided guidance, knowledge, and materials to flesh out this section and all of the historical elements of other sections. They gave us unprecedented access to their archives so we could share them with you.

During our interviews, many people spoke about the museum being a special place, and I found that to be a romantic notion, but didn't take it very seriously, until now. Truly a special place, the museum is where this art form comes together. Not only has ventriloquism grown as an art form, but the museum has grown as well since this documentary was initially released. With a forward thinking curator like Lisa Sweasy, and the steady leadership of Annie Roberts, Brook Brookings and Tom Ladshaw, I know that not only will this amazing institution survive, it will thrive.

How this museum got started is a fantastic story in and of itself. If not for the tenacity of the original caretaking individuals that oversaw Vent Haven, like it's first Board President John R. S. Brooking, this collection may well have been sold off and disappeared, lost forever.

We are honored to be the only people outside the vent community to have their work displayed. There is a unique one of a kind promo poster for *I'm No Dummy* hanging in Building 3 at the museum. In addition, Marge and I spearheaded a program to get touch screens in every building, so visitors could see the vents and their figures performing their art. As of this writing, the museum has gone into an amazing transition period. Two of the old buildings were demolished in September 2021 to make room for a new modern museum. All the profits from our book *I'M NO DUMMY EVERYDAY: 365 Days of Ventriloquial Curiosities, Oddities, and Fun Facts* and this

Vent Haven Museum: IND Promo Poster

book go directly to Vent Haven, supporting this wonderful institution. Marge and I are honored to be on the Board of Advisors for Vent Haven Museum, and as fanatical supporters, we hope everyone gets a chance to visit it.

We have donated all of the raw footage from the shoot for *I'm No Dummy* to the museum. It is archived there for use by future documentarians and journalists. Any fees collected will go straight to the museum.

In addition, we donate a portion of sales from the *I'm No Dummy* documentary to the museum, so thank you for buying the DVD or streaming the film.

The museum's website is: *venthaven.org.*

Stoney Broke at Vent Haven

Vent Haven Founder W. S. Berger's Corner

Is this the end of ventriloquism?

[Tom Ladshaw]: *"Even Paul Winchell understood and could see the light at the end of the tunnel. Or maybe it was the dark at the end of the tunnel, when he said, "Everything can talk." And it can. When a child goes to Disney World and he sees totem poles speaking, again, how is a ventriloquist going to compete with that? They don't even need a ventriloquist."*

Tom Ladshaw

[Jeff Dunham] *"There's some great avenues for this art that are beyond, different from just straight comedy. So I think it will always be here. I hope it will always be here. I hope it doesn't just die away. And I think the more kids that get interested in it the better."*

Peanut and Jeff Dunham

[Lisa Sweasy]: *"I certainly think it's got two lives. There's the archaic version of ventriloquism. The history, particularly the pre-TV history, a lot of people just don't know that."*

The jump cut that I referred to earlier appears in this section. If you watch the film closely, as Lisa speaks, she moves around. I tried also to mask the cut by diverting our eye to the picture-in-picture in the frame.

Lisa Sweasy

[Lisa Sweasy]: *"People are seeing ventriloquists. I mean, there's Jeff Dunham. There's Jay Johnson's Broadway show. There are people who are doing this. So I don't think it's in any peril, as far as dying out forever. But it's an old art form. It's a vaudevillian thing to do. And yet there are these contemporary people who put a whole new life on it. So, no. I don't think it's going anywhere."*

One of the themes in *I'm No Dummy* is "Is ventriloquism an art form?" And certainly, ventriloquism is an art form. The final section wraps up the documentary and answers the second theme of the film, "Is it a dying art form?"

There were varying opinions, but in my opinion Jay Johnson answers it perfectly.

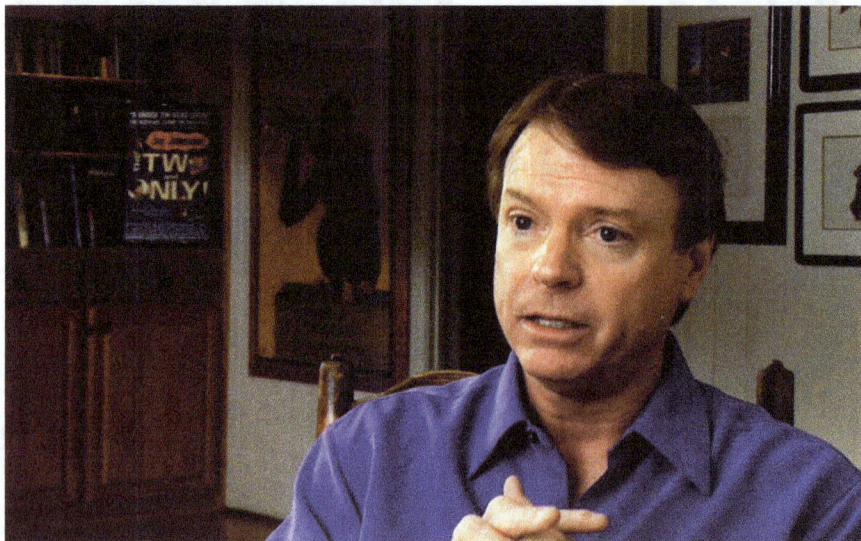

Jay Johnson

[Jay Johnson]: *"But I know it's not a dying art, because art never dies. Art is an expression and we have to stop expressing to kill an art form."*

In screenwriting, the ending of a film is often called "the resolution and future projection," as the story resolves and the future is projected for the characters. I chose to combine a book structure "chapters" with a screenplay structure "acts." This final section, "End of an Era?," is the resolution of our story and the future projection of the art form. But it wasn't until these unique and much maligned performers and their puppet partners opened up to me on camera, in interviews and then in the filming of their live performances, that I recognized their ability to make me feel like an eight-year-old boy again. I went back joyfully to a time when the responsibility of adulthood was so far away, and realized that we all have an inner puppet. They gave me a glimpse into the comic delights and complex creative inventiveness involved in how these vents do what they do. I peeked behind their curtain.

Sailor Jim and Arthur Prince

What started out as a whimsical thought on a long bike ride, ended up as a deconstruction of an obscure art form. And the puppets cut me no slack. They were pretty rough on me. Jeff Dunham's grumpy old man, Walter, called me an "idiot" and refused to answer some of his questions right in the middle of his interview. Jay Johnson's wise ass partner Bob asked me "Are you reading that?," when I referred to my notes. And before I could even

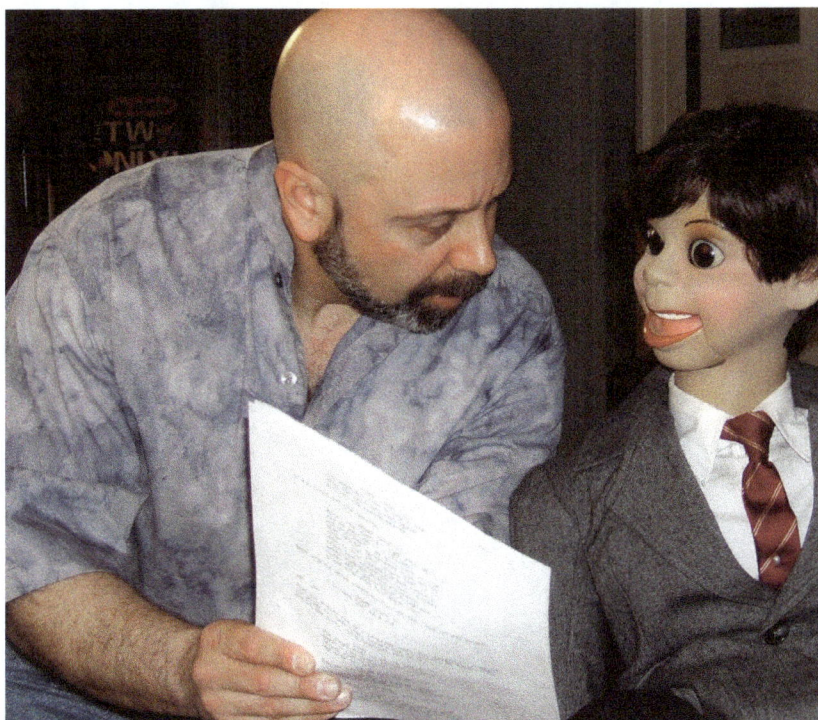

Bryan W. Simon Speaks with Jay Johnson's Partner Bob

start her interview, Lynn Trefzger's partner Emily inquired if I was "available." "Uh, no, my wife's sitting right over there." Being berated has never been more fun. For me the best films inform and entertain, and I don't think I laughed as much making a film as I did on this one.

Each great vent has a style, an approach and a comedy all their own. Jay Johnson wows audiences with his subtly intellectual, rapid-fire exchanges with his partner Bob and his post modern partner, and overbearing monkey, appropriately named Darwin. Lynn Trefzger shares the angst of every modern day parent with her extremely popular puppet three-year-old Chloe.

Jeff Dunham tapped into a post 9/11 zeitgeist with his puppet Achmed, The Dead Terrorist, and muppet on crack partner, Peanut. These and many other vents have taken their art, which is hundreds if not thousands of years old, and turned it on it's head. Sometimes it takes a good ass-kicking by an inanimate object and a trip back to your youth to realize that what you're observing is nothing short of brilliance and that ventriloquism has a past, a present, and will have a future.

When I told our good friend, Producer Christopher Lockhart, something I wanted to include in my director's commentary, he said "Is that before or after they fall asleep?"

Did you make it all the way to the end?

So this is my director's commentary, feel free to contact me through my website, *www.bryanwsimon.com*, if you have any questions or comments.

ORIGINAL END CREDIT CRAWL
(abbreviated):

I'm No Dummy

And the first EMMY AWARD goes to...
A ventriloquist. In 1948, Shirley Dinsdale
and her figure Judy Splinters
won the VERY FIRST Emmy Award.

Written and Directed by
Bryan W. Simon

Of over 90 main stage acts in
Las Vegas, Ronn Lucas is
the only ventriloquist.
He continues to perform daily
at the Luxor Hotel.

Produced by
Marjorie Engesser

Not only was Paul Winchell one of the
finest and most influential ventriloquists,
but he was also the inventor of the artificial
heart,the disposable razor, the plasma bag,
the retractable fountain pen,
and many other inventions.

Executive Producers
Timothy T. Miller
Bryan W. Simon

Terry Fator, a ventriloquist, was the
winner of NBC's hit reality show,
AMERICA'S GOT TALENT.
He won one million dollars.

Director of Photography
Lloyd Freidus

Ventriloquists Shari Lewis and Mallory Lewis are the only mother-daughter team to ever win an Emmy award.

Edited by Bryan W. Simon
with Larry Stewart

Jeff Dunham continues to be a star in the vent and comedy world. His DVD's have sold millions of copies, his TV specials continue to break records, and he sells out concert halls and performance arenas throughout the country.

Music by
Elliot Anders

Nearly 30 years after starring on the ground breaking hit TV sitcom SOAP, Jay Johnson became the first ventriloquist to win a Tony Award® for his ventriloquial Broadway show JAY JOHNSON: THE TWO AND ONLY! Currently he is touring the world with his show.

Associate Producer
Tom Ladshaw

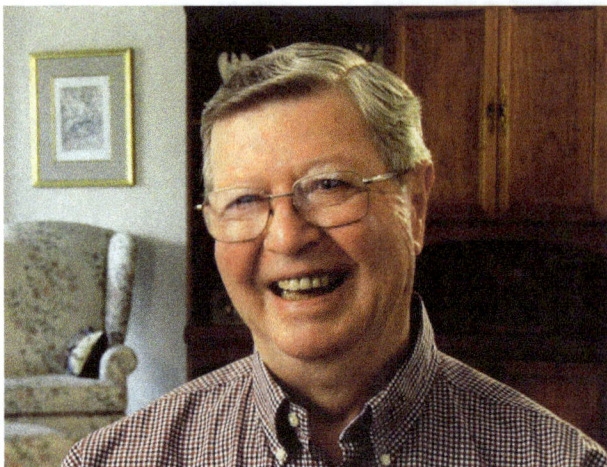

And Jimmy Nelson continues to perform to this day. Why? Because his phone still rings.

With

Kelly Asbury
Allan Blumenstyk
Burt Dubrow
Jeff Dunham
Dr. David Goldblatt
Ken Groves
Jay Johnson
Mary Kingsley
Tom Ladshaw
Mallory Lewis
Ronn Lucas
Jimmy Nelson
Norm Nielsen
Otto Petersen
Stevo Schüling
Lisa Sweasy
Lynn Trefzger
Willie Tyler
Vonda Kay Van Dyke

Sound Design
Elliot Anders

Second Camera
Eric Stewart

Legal Services
Donaldson & Hart
Michael C. Donaldson
Marja M. Lopees
and
Dennis Angel, Esq.

Film Consultant
Thomas Ethan Harris

Digital Intermediate by
PlasterCITY Digital Post, L.L.C.

DI Colorists
Milton Adamou

DI Supervisor
Michael Cioni

Post Producer
Paul Geffre

Re-recording Mixer
Glen Alger Schricker

Jeff Dunham was filmed live at
The Improv Comedy Club & Dinner Theatre
Irvine, CA

Lakewood Civic Auditorium
Cleveland, OH

Jay Johnson was filmed live at the
Hermosa Beach Comedy & Magic Club
Hermosa Beach, CA

Lynn Trefzger was filmed live at the
Cerritos Center for the Performing Arts
Cerritos, CA

You can find more wonderful
information about the golden era of
ventriloquism in Kelly Asbury's
fascinating book "Dummy Days".
Available through Amazon.com
or your local bookstores.

In Memory of
Jeri Whitson
1928 - 2008
You brought out the artist in us.

www.montivagus.com
www.montivaguspress.com

About the Author

Bryan W. Simon never thought he would direct a movie or write a book about ventriloquism. A screenwriters' strike changed all that, inspiring him to rediscover an art form that reawakened his inner child. An award-winning and critically acclaimed director, writer, and visualist, some of Simon's feature films include the smash hit comedy documentary *I'm No Dummy*, the first feature length film on ventriloquism; the big screen adaptation of the Tony® Award winning Broadway show, *Jay Johnson: The Two & Only!*; and the indie darling, *Along For The Ride*. He has written the coffee table/calendar book *I'M NO DUMMY EVERYDAY: 365 Days of Ventriloquial Oddities, Curiosities, and Fun Facts* as well as articles on filmmaking for *MovieMaker* magazine, *No Film School*, *The Wrap*, and others. He has been a guest instructor in directing and filmmaking at various universities and colleges and was the co-producer of the educational seminar series at the American Cinematheque in Hollywood. In addition, Bryan was the Founder and Artistic Director for the Chicago area Stage Two Theatre Company. Bryan and his wife, film producer Marjorie Engesser, proudly serve on the Vent Haven Museum Board of Advisors.

Visit his website at: www.bryanwsimon.com

V·H·M

VENT HAVEN MUSEUM

www.venthaven.org

Your purchase of this book directly supports VENT HAVEN MUSEUM...

the only museum in the world dedicated to the art of ventriloquism.

ALSO Available on Amazon:

I'M NO DUMMY EVERYDAY
365 Days of Ventriloquial Oddities,
Curiosities, and Fun Facts

A must have for show business fans in general and ventriloquism fans in particular, *I'm No Dummy Everyday* is the perfect coffee table book. Devour the engaging and entertaining tidbits all in one sitting OR check out a fun fact each day of the week. Tons of terrific photographs and images are provided for sharing with family and friends.

All profits go directly to Vent Haven!

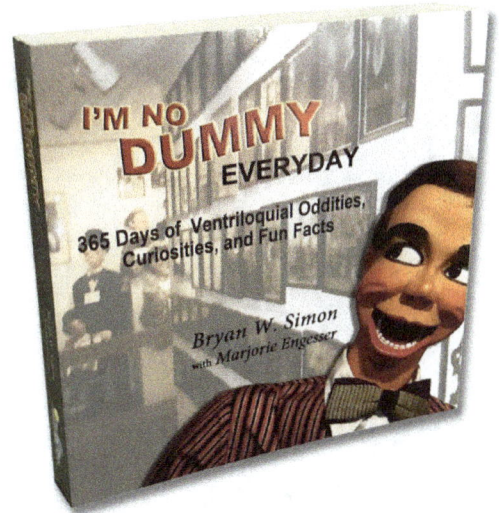

Join us on our *I'm No Dummy* FACEBOOK page with clips, trivia, and more.

With Special Thanks for Encouragement and Support

Sheryl Scarborough
Jerry Piat

Jay Johnson

Mary Alvarado

Tom Ladshaw
Lisa Sweasy
Annie Roberts

Christopher Lockhart

ON THE FRONT COVER:

A René Zendejas figure. The head sits on a walking body which was created by René for Jay Johnson's partner Bob on the sitcom *SOAP* so Bob could roller skate.

Full Transcription of...

I'm No Dummy

A documentary about venting
By Bryan W. Simon

Peanut
I'm no dummy! Wait a minute. I'm no dummy! Oh, crap!

Lamb Chop
Dummy? I'm no dummy! Poo-ey!

Farfel
I'm no dummy.

Buffalo Billy
I'm no dummy.

Jay
You just say, "I'm no dummy"?

Bob
I don't want to say that. I'm not a dummy?

Jay
That's what you're saying, "I'm not a..."

Bob
Well that's the implication. If you say you're not a dummy, that means you are.

Peanut
I'm no dummy! I don't know. Can I start over?

Señor Wences
Very difficult.

Johnnie
Easy.

Wences
Easy? No, no, no. Very confusing.

Walter
I'm no d- I'm no... I'm do d- uh, uh. Shit. I can't say it. I'm no... I don't know.

Danny O'Day
Timber!

Ed Sullivan
Unfortunately.

Darwin
I'm not a dummy. I'm a monkey. A monkey!

Emily
I'm no dummy. But I am available.

Achmed
Silence! I kill you.
Wences
So kay?

Pedro
So right.

Wences
All right.

Hiam
Ani lo buba.

Jay
It's the name of the show. You say, "I'm no..." What could be hard about that?

Bob
Well, you don't understand it.

Jay
Just say it.

Bob
I don't want to.

Danny
Down boy. Down boy. Say something. Say something.

Charlie
Say it!

Scorch
I'm no dummy.

Camelot
I just need a drink. I'm no dummy.

Lester
I'm no dummy.

Jay
If I say it, will you say it?

Bob
Sure.

Jay
Okay, I say, I'm no dummy.

Bob
No, that doesn't work.

Jay
You say it.

Bob
You say it with me.

Jay
With you?

Bob
Yeah.

Jay
Can we do that?

Bob
Yeah.

Jay
All right. On three, we'll both say "I'm no dummy" together, okay?

Bob
Yeah.

Jay
Okay here we go. One...

Bob
Two.

Jay Johnson
Three. I'm...

Bob
No...

What's Ventriloquism ?

Jeff Dunham
I think to define ventriloquism, it's a guy who throws his voice or makes the voice appear from some other source. But, for me, I don't like to be labeled just that. My goal is to just make the audience laugh. And make them want to come back and see a show again. And bring their friends.

(Clip begins from the Improv, Irvine, CA)

Walter
Hey, is that a new watch?

Jeff
I've had this forever.

Walter
Oh. I remember a long time ago you used to have an ugly black plastic thing. It had a funny name.

Jeff
That was years ago when I was in college. How do you remember that? They were popular then, it was called a Swatch.

Walter
A what?

Jeff
A Swatch.

Walter
What the hell is a Swatch?
Jeff
I don't know, some company in Switzerland invented that kind of watch so they called it a Swatch?

Walter
Oh, good thing they weren't in Croatia. What time is it? I don't know

74

let me look at my Crotch. Sorry I'm late, my Crotch is a little slow.
Yes, it's like a Timex, it takes a lick...

Jeff
WALTER!

(Clip ends from the Improv, Irvine, CA)

Lamb Chop
Ven-tril-o-quism is the art and science of making the person standing next to
you look like they're talking without moving your lips.

Bob
Oh, yeah, ventriloquism. I think it's the subversion of the masses.
The wooden people should strike against ventriloquism because, you know,
we could be doing other things...

Jay
Bob, Bob, just stick to it.

Bob
Okay. Okay. Ventriloquism, a nice way to make a living. I'd rather do this
than be a chair. Ha, ha, ha. Did it work the second time?

Jay
Big time.

Peanut
I would like to define the word ventriloquism.

Jeff
You can do that?

Peanut
Oh, sure. I think it's some kind of French word.

Jeff
Latin.

Peanut
Latin word. Ventra- meaning... Uh.. Yeah...

Jeff
What is it?

Peanut
I don't know. No. Ask Jay Johnson.

Jay
Well, for me, ventriloquism is the art form of acting and reacting within
the same word, much less the same scene.

(Clip begins from the Comedy and Magic Club, Redondo Beach, CA)

Bob
Are you doing your job now, Jay?

Jay
Yeah, I'm doing my job.

Bob
Wow. This is work?

Jay
It is to me. Yeah, yes it is.

Bob
How do you know when you're done?

Jay
Well, you know what, I... I throw my voice.

Bob
Good, good, good. You gonna throw some tonight, Jay?

Jay
What?

Bob
You gonna do it tonight? You gonna throw your voice? You gonna do your thing?
Is that what you're gonna do, Jay?

Jay
Right then. That's when I do it.

Bob
What?

Jay
That's what I do, right there.

Bob
Huh?

Jay
Yup. That's it.

Bob
What?

Jay
Right here.

Bob
You do it now?

Jay
Not now.

Bob
When?

Jay
Right there.

Jay
But not now. See, by the time you do it, I'm done.

Bob
What?

Jay
Did it again.

Bob
Huh?

Jay
There it is.

Bob
Huh?

Jay
There. Right there.

Bob
Huh?

Jay
There.

Bob
Wait a minute!

Jay
All right.

Bob
You don't...! Don't say nothing!
Don't say nothing, Jaaaay.

Jay
I better get back to work and earn a living. Here I go. Any second...
...now. Here it comes. Here it is.

Bob
Where?

Jay
There. Right there.

Bob
There.

Jay
That's it. That's it. I talk for you. That is my job. I'm not
particularly proud of it. That's what I do.

Bob
Save it! Save it! Save it! He's got a weak finish.

Jay
Okay. Stop it, stop it.

(Clip ends from the Comedy and Magic Club, Redondo Beach, CA)

Mary Kingsley
It's just the ability to communicate comedy or whatever thoughts you have through
another, another being. Hopefully, over which you have control.

Lynn Trefzger
It's a way of expressing different sides of my personality.

Norm Nielsen
Ventriloquism, I think, it's that ability to create life in an inanimate object.

(Clip from "Who's In Charge Here?" – 1988)

[Kazoo sound]

Ronn Lucas
That's a lousy idea. Ladies and gentlemen...

[Kazoo sound]

Ronn
One of the problems we've had in the past.

[Kazoo sound]

(Clip ends from "Who's In Charge Here?" – 1988)

Camelot
Ventric-- Ventrilli-Ventri-- That's a guy who dresses like a girl. Isn't that it?

Lynn
No. It's what I do.

Camelot
Your what?

Lynn
It's what I do. I'm a ventriloquist. And you are?

Camelot
Huh?

Lynn
And you are?

Camelot
Drunk.

Lynn
You are what?

Camelot
Animal.

Lynn
Yes. But you're my puppet.

(Clip of Lynn Trefzger on stage)
Lynn
Aw, I tell you what. John, if you could stand there. If you could be my babysitter,
I'd really appreciate it cause I have to get Jed. Okay? Thank you.

[Baby cries]

Lynn
John. Wrong end.

Allan Blumenstyk
Giving a character another life aside from yourself. So it's not just speaking,
it's what you are speaking. And how you are speaking it and how you are conveying
what you want to say through yourself and through your figure.

Hiam
Ventriloquism is actually someone talking without moving his lips. For example,
look at this. Now I'm talking and I'm not moving my lips at all. Isn't it great?
That's what it is.

Walter
I have no idea what the exact meaning of the word is. I do
know it's a very sad profession.

Jeff
A what?

Walter
A sad stinking profession. I've got nothing else to do in my life so I know –
I'll be a ventriloquist. How sad.

Lisa Sweasy
I think ventriloquism is a fabulous illusion. And a good ventriloquist is the most
believable thing in the world. I like to watch a vent who's got this distinct
alter ego or this other character that they're doing.

(Clip begins from Ed Sullivan's "Toast of the Town" – 1949)

Jerry Mahoney
(Singing)
We hope that you liked our act and as a matter of fact, you know,
we're really in love with you. Just sing.

Paul Winchell
Me?

Jerry
Yeah.

Paul
(Singing)
We really think that you're great.

Jerry
That's right.

Paul
(Singing)
And as an audience you rate.

Jerry
Go ahead.

Paul
(Singing)
An orchid from Jerry.

79

Jerry
And who?

Paul
(Singing)
And me.

Jerry
Very good.

Jerry
(Singing)
But right now there is something much more important. You tell them kid.

(Clip ends from Ed Sullivan's "Toast of the Town" – 1949)

Lisa Sweasy
To me it's a, It's a monologue that has to be perceived as a dialogue or it's no good.

Stevo Schüling
Very much a focus through which I can see life and our times.

Dr. David Goldblatt
Ventriloquism really becomes this paradigm case of being beside one's self, and
it's talking to one's self in some strange way. And it has this kind of double act
in which the audience becomes involved to see the act as two people in
conversation as well as one person talking to himself.

(Clip begins from the Comedy and Magic Club, Redondo Beach, CA)

Jay Johnson
(muffled)
Forget the whole thing.

Bob
(muffled)
Huh?

Jay
(muffled)
Forget the whole thing.

Bob
(muffled)
Huh?

Jay
(Bob's voice)
Forget the whole thing. I'm not going to do it because...

Bob
(Jay's voice)
Something's wrong here.

Jay
(Bob's voice)
Wait a minute.

Bob
(Jay's voice)

Oh, my god.

Jay
(Bob's voice)
What happened?

Bob
(Jay's voice)
I don't know. I said hello, hello and I got stuck like this.

Jay
(Bob's voice)
That's my voice.

Bob
(Jay's voice)
That's mine.

Jay
(Bob's voice)
Give it back.

Bob
(Jay's voice)
I didn't take it.

Jay
(Bob's voice)
I feel stupid.

Bob
(Jay's voice)
You look kinda natural, Jaaaaay.

(Clip ends from the Comedy and Magic Club, Redondo Beach, CA)

Why Vent ?

Lynn
I felt very comfortable having a puppet. I think part of, you know,
my personality came out through the puppet. The attention was taken off of me
and put on the puppet. On the dummy. I think that's how it kinda took off.

(Clip of Lynn age 14 with Uncle Johnny and Simon)

Lynn Trefzger
Hello, Uncle Johnny.

Uncle Johnny
Hello.

Lynn
Uncle Johnny?

Uncle Johnny
Yes.

Lynn
Well, how did you get here today?
Uncle Johnny. How did I get here?

Simon
Yeah, Uncle Johnny how did you get here?

Uncle Johnny
I drove my car.

Lynn
You drove your what?

Simon
You drove your what?

Uncle Johnny
I drove my car.

Simon
He drove his car.

Lynn
You drove your car.

Uncle Johnny
I drove my car.

Simon
That's what he said. He drove his car.

(Clip ends of Lynn age 14 with Uncle Johnny and Simon)

(Clip begins of Lynn and Emily)

Emily
Hello. Slice me a hunk of that.

Lynn
Emily.

Emily
Hi. What's your name? What's your name? Mike. Such a strong manly name.
Here's a mike, too. So, do you go to school, Mike? Uh, huh, what are you studying?
Besides me. Teaching. That's so sexy. What school do you-- - Oh! Camera.

Lynn
Okay. Okay. Emily.

Emily
Hold it!

Lynn
What?

Emily
There's a girl.

Lynn
Yeah?

Emily
She's sitting right next to him.

Lynn
It's okay.

Emily
He's mine!

Lynn
Emily.

Emily
Tramp!

Lynn
Hey! Sorry. I'm sorry. You apologize. You apologize.

Emily
I'm sorry. That you're a tramp.

Lynn
Emily!

Emily
Sorry.

Lynn
Nicely.

Emily
Ha!

Lynn
Okay. What is with you?

Emily
I'm just getting in touch with my inner bitch.

Lynn
Okay.

(Clip ends with Lynn and Emily)

Jeff Dunham
I grew up in Dallas, Texas. And an only child. It's so sad. It's so sad to say that
when you're a ventriloquist. Sadly enough, this little ventriloquism thing came along.
And I would get up in front of the class and I would get laughs. And I suddenly |
had more friends. As a kid I was a horrible athlete. My parents made me
play basketball. Baseball. Soccer. I was on all those teams. And I was the last one.
Nobody wanted me on the field. It was something that was great for me.
Because as this shy little kid, I now had something that I was good at. And I just
kept doing it. There was no reason to quit. And, I guess what motivated me
was more success. And, just the accolades. And, The family saying it was funny.
So, I don't know. Either everybody's been lying to me for a long time,
or they actually think the little guys are funny.

(Clip begins from Jeff Dunham's "Spark of Insanity" tour)

Peanut
You know I think I'd be cool to be a ventriloquist.

Jeff
You think so?

Peanut
I'd throw my voice everywhere.

Jeff
Like what?

Peanut
I'd go to a lot of funerals. Oh, think how much fun you could have.
Dearly beloved we are gathered here today. I'm not dead yet. Let me outta here.
You son of a bitch. You know where else I'd throw my voice?

Jeff
Where?

Peanut
On the airline.

Jeff
The airline?

Peanut
[Drunk voice]
This is your captain speaking. Boy, are we having fun flying big airplane.
We're sorry about the turbulence. So you better keep your seat belt fastened
and if you don't Co-Captain Bob is going to back there and kick your ass.
Thanks for flying the friendly skies.

(Clip ends from Jeff Dunham's "Spark of Insanity" tour)

Willie Tyler
Yeah, I wanted to be popular, but I was kind of shy and withdrawn. By seeing
the Paul Winchell Show on television, and watching the Ed Sullivan shows.
I liked that. So I figured, well maybe I can do that. Like, you know? Like the Lone Ranger
would always wear masks so you couldn't recognize him. I figured the character,
the ventriloquist character, would be my mask. I could act silly and stuff like that.
And I figured I'd take that other personality of mind and put it through that character.
And that way I would be known through the neighborhood. And it worked.

(Clip begins from The David Letterman Show - 2007)

Willie Tyler
Thank you. This part of the show, we're gonna give them what they
call "the hambone". This is what, I'll give the folks this.
(Stomps foot and slaps side of pants)
And you do the words, right?

Lester
Right.

Willie
When you finish with the words?

Lester
Yeah?

Willie
I'll come back and I'll do this. I'll go- And then, you know what? I'll add this.

I'll go- [Knocking sound] Now while I'm doing those two things.

Lester
Uh-huh?

Willie
I want you to hum at the same time.

Lester
I gotta see this.

Willie
We've got to move it now. We've got to go fast.

Lester
Yeah.

Willie
Ready?

Lester
This I gotta see.

Willie
Okay, ready? Go. Here we go.

Lester
Went to try out for a play. Didn't take long, just all day. Well, the final words
were toodle-loo. Don't call us, we won't call you.

Willie
Now here are. Get ready. Get ready. Go!
[Knocking sound] Come on. Come on!

Lester
[Humming Sound]

(Clip ends from The David Letterman Show - 2007)

Jay Johnson
Acute dyslexia. I don't think I'm, um, uh- I guess on a scale of one to ten
I'm probably a seven or eight. So I'm not- It's not a huge burden.
But it caused me to not deal with school well. I didn't do well on tests.
I didn't do well- It was an attempt to do something that I thought I could
excel at. To compete. And it was unusual. So it wasn't like I was competing
with a lot of people when I did that. So, yeah. Probably, an answer to
the question you asked before, how did you become a ventriloquist,
that's probably it. Why did you become a dyslexic?
I don't know. But it probably caused me to be a ventriloquist.

(Clip begins from the Comedy and Magic Club, Redondo Beach, CA)

Bob
I don't care, Jay! I don't care, Jay! (To audience)I think they're looking at
me like they don't believe me at all. You're thinking I'm not real, aren't you?
You think he's doing that. That's what he does.
That's not true. It's not true. You ever seen those Chucky movies? Ahhhh.

Jay
All right, stop it! Stop it. Stop it.

Bob
I don't care. I don't care. I don't care, Jay. Yes, indeed.

Jay
You like it here?

Bob
I do! I do. It's a nice place.

Jay
Yeah?

Bob
Yep.

Jay
You can dig it?

Bob
Yep.

Jay
Yep?

Bob
Yep. That's not the correct... That's not what I was looking for.

Bob
I don't care what you're looking for. I don't care. I told you. I don't need the job.

Jay
I know that. When I said "Can you dig it?", I wanted you to say "I can dig it."

Bob
How do you say it?

Jay
Well, to conjugate the verb correctly, I say, "Can you dig it?"
And you go, "Well, I can dig it."

Bob
How do you say it?

Jay
I can dig it.

Bob
How?

Jay
I.
Bob
I.

Jay
Can.

Bob
Can.

Jay
Dig.

Bob
Dig.

Jay
It.

Bob
It.

Jay
That's it. Now try that. You like it here?

Bob
Yeah.

Jay
Can you dig it?

Bob
I can dug it.

Jay
Not dug it. It's dig it.

Bob
How do you say it?

Jay
Dig it.

Jay
Dug it.

Jay
Dig it.
Bob
How do you spell it?

Jay
D-I-G I-T. Dig. Not dug. Now, if you're going to talk to me, then
you say "Can you dig it?"

Bob
Can you dig it?

Jay
I say I can dig it. Got it.

Bob
Got it.

Jay
And if you're talking about someone else, it's the third person.
Yeah. If it's a guy, you say "He can dig it." If it's a girl, you say
"She can dig it." If it's all of us, we say "We can..."

Bob
I don't care, I ain't doing it!

Jay
Come on. You can do it.

Bob
I can do it?

Jay
Sure. Try it.

Bob
Try it?

Jay
Try it.

Bob
Yeah, okay. I can try it. I can dig it.

Jay
Right.

Bob
You can dig it.

Jay
Right.

Bob
She can dig it. They can dig it. We can dig it. I got it. Okay.

Jay
All right. Now, I say the pronoun and you finish it up with
the proper tense of the verb.

Bob
I'm very tense.

Jay
I know you are. Here we are. Yeah. Ready?

Bob
Yeah.

Jay
Here we go. I.

Bob
I can dig it!

Jay
Right. You.

Bob
You can dig it.

Jay
She.

Bob
She can dig it.

Jay
They.
Bob
They can dig it.

Jay
We.

Bob
We can dig it.

Jay
He.

Bob
He can dig it.

Jay
You.

Bob
You can dig it.

Jay
They.

Bob
You, she, they, we, you, she, they, we, you, she....

Jay
Hold it.

Bob
Dig it. Dig it. Dig it,

Jay
Hold it. Hold it.

Bob
Dig it, dig it, dig…

Jay
Hold it. Hold it! What happened?

Bob
You ran out of air.

Jay
Okay. All right.

(Clip ends from the Comedy and Magic Club, Redondo Beach, CA)

Don't Move Your Lips !

(Clip begins from "The Dick Van Dyke Show" – 1963)

Rob Petrie
Well, what do you do, Mel?

Melvin Cooley
Well, I, uh- Uh- Fool around with, uh... Ventriloquism.

Rob
What?

Mel
Ventriloquism.

Rob
Ventriloquism?

Mel
Hello, Dummy.

Dummy
Hello, Mr. Cooley.

Mel
How are you?

Dummy
I'm fine.

Mel
What's new with you, Dummy?

Dummy
Well, Mr. Cooley. I'm in love.

Mel
How could you be in love? You have no poise. No charm. No savoir faire.

Dummy
Jimmy crack corn and I don't care. Jimmy crack corn and I don't care.

Rob
Mel?

Dummy
Jimmy crack corn and I don't care!

Rob
I think we probably- We get the general idea, I think.

Mel
Oh, well thank you, Rob.

Dummy
Thank you, Rob.

Mel
Well. What about it?

Rob
Well, it's... That's very funny, Mel. Of course you realize your lips move a little bit?

Mel
Well, they're better than they used to be.

(Clip ends from "The Dick Van Dyke Show" – 1963)

Stevo Schüling
Lip control is the one most important obvious thing about ventriloquism.

Ed Sullivan
The greatest ventriloquist, you can't detect any action at all. Jimmy Nelson
from Chicago. Let's have a nice welcome.

Jummy Nelson
When I started out, lip control was very, very important to me.

(Clip begins from "The Ed Sullivan Show" – 1950)

Danny O'Day
Ah, ventriloquists smiliquists, what can you do?

Jimmy Nelson
Well, I can say the letter "M" without moving my lips.

Danny
That's hard?

Jimmy
That's hard.

Danny
I've got news for you kid.

Jimmy
What's that?

Danny
I can do that too.

Jimmy
You can say the letter "M" without moving your lips?

Danny
That's right.

Jimmy
Let's see it.

Danny
You wanna see me? Well now watch me.

Jimmy
I'm watching.

Danny
Don't let it get away.

Jimmy
What are you waiting for?

Danny
I'm waiting for you, you Schmo.

(Clip ends from "The Ed Sullivan Show" – 1950)

Jimmy
Now, as I get older, I find it's harder for me as I could as a youngster, to keep those lips perfectly still. It gets harder as you get older. No matter how much you practice.

Ronn Lucas
And of course, you have a distraction. You have a character whose mouth is moving. And of all of our senses, our hearing is our least sensitive. So, we tend to look, believe it or not, using our eyes for sounds sources. So if a ventriloquist is sitting there and his face and throat don't seem to be moving and the puppet's mouth is moving, your whole attention goes there. It's psychology.

Otto Petersen
There's something about performing on TV that makes your eye go to the ventriloquist's mouth. And you're examining his technique, rather than listening to what the guy is saying. In a nightclub the illusion is perfect. Where people just- I'll look at the first row of the audience and they'll just be staring at George with t his stupid grin on their face, or laughing, but not even looking at me. But there' something about television that makes it- I don't know. You study it. You examine the flaws more.

Ken Groves
As soon as the audience hears there's going to be a ventriloquist, they have certain expectations of what they're about to see. A lot of times they're not good expectations because there are so many bad ventriloquists. But they expect somebody that can talk without moving their lips. They expect somebody that can create the illusion of two people on stage at once.

Jeff
I think a good ventriloquist is able to carry on a conversation with himself. But the only thing he's done is tapped into that inner voice. Because all of us, I think, sit there and go, "All right, I'm gonna do this. No. Maybe... Uh, I don't know. Maybe I shouldn't, maybe I should." So that's all that you're doing with yourself. Is, you're taking that dialogue and turning it into an outside thing.

(Clip begins from the Improv, Irvine, CA)

Walter
What are you shaking your head at? You got a good love life?

Jeff Dunham
Yeah.

Walter
Oh. Good sex life?

Jeff
Yeah.

Walter
With your wife?

Jeff
Yes.

92

Walter
Is it good for her too?

Jeff
Well, yeah.
Walter
How do you know?

Jeff
What?

Walter
How do you know? We're waiting.

Jeff
Well, sometimes she calls me the hurricane.

Walter
The what?

Jeff
The hurricane.

Walter
Oh, yeah! I get it. Exciting at first, then it ends in disaster.

(Clip ends from the Improv, Irvine, CA)

Jay Johnson
I think of it as, I always describe it as a big triangle. And you've got lip control.
And you've got animation and characterization. And what you want is them to
come right together at the exact right point. But, it still forms a triangle.
If one of them is a little bit longer than the other and this is shorter.
So if you're not quite as good lip control but fantastic characterization,
that would still form that triangle where that moment is performing.

Jeff Dunham
How many different aspects there are with what the ventriloquist does.
You're an actor. You're a comedian. You're a puppeteer. I mean there
are just so many things that go into it.

(Clip begins from The Cerritos Center for the Performing Arts)

Chloe
Can I have gum?

Lynn Trefzger
No. Chloe, come on. What happened the last time you had gum?

Chloe
I swallowed it.

Lynn
Yes. What happens when you swallow gum?

Chloe
It takes a long time to come out the other end.

Lynn
Yeah.

Chloe
I think my mommy swallowed a lot of gum when she was little.

Lynn
Why?

Chloe
She thinks she has a bubble butt.

Lynn
Your mommy's having a baby.

Chloe
Uh-huh!

Lynn
What do you want, a brother or a sister?

Chloe
I want a puppy.

Lynn
Okay.

Chloe
I know where babies come from.

Lynn
You do?

Chloe
Babies R Us. You go in and pick one out and you put
it in your cart. And you can't take it back.

Lynn
No?

Chloe
Even if it's ugly.

Lynn
Okay.

Chloe
And some people get two babies.
Lynn
Two babies?

Chloe
You have to have a coupon.

Lynn
Oh.

Chloe
And some people get three babies.

Lynn
Three babies?

Chloe
You've got to go to Costco.

(Clip ends from The Cerritos Center for the Performing Arts)

Dr. David Glodblatt
And the very idea that there is this kind of relationship between a person and
an inanimate object, I think is really what, you know - What we're basically targeting.
And it's because of this that the audience, which sits there as a kind of witness
or kind of judge, you know? Are the lips moving? You know? And I think
that it's not so much the lips moving, but is the personality exchange
going seamlessly? And I think that's what really makes the best of the
ventriloquists. The idea of that seamless exchange, of that one can switch those
personalities or characters between myself and the dummy very quickly.
And I think that becomes intriguing.

(Clip begins from "Jay Johnson: The Two & Only!" – 2007)

Darwin
Where are the bars?

Jay
There's no bars.

Darwin
You're not in a cage.

Jay
I wanted a drink!

Jay
What'll you have?

Darwin
A banana daiquiri. Banana daiquiri! That's a monkey joke!

Jay
Okay. I think I got it.

Darwin
Cause I'm a monkey.

Jay
They know that.

Darwin
I do monkey jokes.

Jay
They understand that.

Darwin
Cause I'm a monkey.

Jay
They know that.

Darwin
Simian satire. Rhesus rhetoric. Monkey mon- Stay with me!

95

Jay
All right. Leave them alone, please.

Darwin
Don't make me come down there.

Jay
Leave them alone, please.

Darwin
I'll show a matinee.

Jay
Hey, hey, hey, hey.

(Clip ends from "Jay Johnson: The Two & Only!" – 2007)

There's Two of Us Here !

Jeff Dunham
If I believe onstage that these guys are carrying on a conversation with me
and are actually real, that audience is easily sucked into that reality as well.
But then every once in awhile I have to throw in something to break
that wall down and go, "Look, you people. This is all fake.
You realize I am arguing with myself?"

(Clip begins from Jeff Dunham's "Spark of Insanity" tour)

Jeff
What did you do on our time off?

Walter
Usually I went back to the hotel and got on the internet.

Jeff
What?

Walter
What?

Jeff
What?

Walter
What do you mean what?

Jeff
What?

Walter
You actually don't know what I just said? Does anyone else find this a bit odd?
Do you really think you're that good? That you no longer have to pay any attention
to what the hell you're making me say? You're a sick man. You need some help.

(Clip ends from Jeff Dunham's "Spark of Insanity" tour)

Jay
But the genius of that is that you never want the audience to forget how hard

you're working at that. Because the tendency is that if you're so good, they suddenly think of you as two people. And then you're judged on what two people can or can't do. You must continually remind them that this is me doing this. I have fooled you. And that brings you back to that, "Oh, I'm back to reality! Oh, oh!" Then you breakthat reality again and you go, "Oh, that's right. He's just doing that." And that becomes your comedy arc. That becomes your way to get back to it. That's the way to remind the audience that this is ventriloquism, not, you know, two stand-ups. This is reminding them that they've been fooled.

(Clip begins from "The Ed Sullivan Show" with Arthur Worsley and Charlie Brown - 1958)

Charlie Brown
Say "a bottle of beer" without moving your mouth. Go on.
Say "a bottle of beer"! Without moving your mouth. Say it! Say it!
How is it son that when I shout, you spit in my face? Say it! Say it!
A bottle of beer! A bottle of beer! A bottle of beer! A bottle of beer!
A bottle of beer! A bottle of beer! A bottle of beer! A bottle of beer!
You can't do it, can you?

(Clip ends from "The Ed Sullivan Show" - 1958)

Jimmy Nelson
I used to do a cigarette smoking routine.

(Clip begins from "The Ed Sullivan Show" - 1950)

Danny O'Day
[Humming]

(Clip ends from "The Ed Sullivan Show" - 1950)

Jimmy
Not to reveal the ventriloquist side of it, Danny suddenly says,
"I can do that trick too.
I can smoke a cigarette and make you talk."

(Clip begins from "The Ed Sullivan Show" - 1950)

Danny
(Singing)
The robins that sing. Someday the child... Look, this is silly.

Jimmy
Continue.

Danny
(singing)
They're yours. They're mine. Well, thank you, Doris Day.

Jimmy
Never mind

(Clip ends from "The Ed Sullivan Show" - 1950)

Dr. David Goldblatt
And that kind of breaks that illusion for the moment so that the audience becomes aware that, in some sense, they're responsible. The choice is there to see it this way or see it, you know, another way.

Stevo Schüling
And I call that "to rip the curtain". To make the audience aware that, hey.
This is an illusion. This is just a play. And you want to be fooled.
You enjoy being fooled.

(Clip begins from The Cerritos Center for the Performing Arts)

Lynn Trefzger
Are you going to sing? Yes, go ahead.

Camelot
I don't know what to sing.

Lynn
All right, I have a song for you.
Camelot
Huh?

Lynn
How about, um- How about "You Are My Sunshine"? Do you know it?

Camelot
Do you?

Lynn
Yes.

Camelot
Then I do.

Lynn
Just sing it.

Camelot
Don't worry. That'll sink in later. What's your name again?
Yeah. Am I looking at him?

Lynn
Yes.

Camelot
Yes. What is your name? Phillip. Phillip! Pay attention.

Lynn
Sorry.

(Clip ends from The Cerritos Center for the Performing Arts)

Tom Ladshaw
There is not only the suspension of disbelief, but the suspension
of belief there on the puppet's part.

Simon
Will you think of something.

Lynn
I'm sorry.

Simon
I sound like an idiot.

Lynn
I'm sorry.

Jay Johnson
Always remind them that you're doing it. You know? It's funny,
but it's so... It's such depth of reality. I love it.

What's SOAP Got to Do With It ?

Tom Ladshaw
Everyone became aware of Jay Johnson in the late seventies when
he appeared on SOAP. And all of a sudden, overnight, ventriloquism was
visible again. And not only was it visible, but it
was on a show that, at the time, was not only hip but really edgy.

Lynn Trefzger
A couple times there, my parents would get me up from bed and say,
"Jay Johnson's on!" He was on "Soap". So I was only allowed to watch
his part and then I had to go to bed. Cause, you know, it was too mature
for me. So. And I'll never forget that.
They're like, "Come on, Lynn! There's a ventriloquist on!"

Jay Johnson
When I came to Los Angeles, the idea of being on
a sitcom called "Soap", or any sitcom where
I would play a ventriloquist, was about as far away from - I mean,
I couldn't even fantasize about that. That had never been done before.

(Clip begins from SOAP – 1977)

Chuck
(Singing)
Hello!

Bob
(Singing)
Hello!

Chuck
We're here to start the show! I'm Chuck.

Bob
I'm Bob. Hello, hello, hello!

Chuck
Let's go, let's go, let's go! I'll sing and dance!

Bob
He'll dance and sing! Wherever we go.

Chuck
Whatever we do.

Bob
We're gonna go through it together, yeah!

(Clip ends from SOAP – 1977)

Jay
Jay Sandrich, the director of "Soap", decided that they couldn't do that part as
originally planned with an actor and they would just loop the voice in. And that's
when they started looking for a ventriloquist. But in that audition for "Soap"
I took Squeaky. Squeaky was my character. And so, the first couple of days
of doing "Soap" I used Squeaky. Until they introduced me to what would
become Bob. And would become my partner for really the rest of my life.
Uh, I had no idea about that. I had no idea why we would need to have
a different character. But they were looking at it as casting. They cast me.
I was perfect for Chuck. But they were also going to cast Bob.

(Clip ends from "Jay Johnson: The Two & Only!" – 2007)

Squeaky
Well, you got the part.

Jay
Yeah. But see, they also told me - The agent told me that they don't, um-

Squeaky
What?
Jay
They don't think that you're right to play this "Bob".

Squeaky
Well, didn't... Didn't they like what I did?

Jay
No, they liked your audition. It wasn't about your acting ability.
They think you're a very good actor. They said...? It's all about the look.

Squeaky
What?

Jay
See, he's- Bob's a really mean character. And they don't
think you look right to play the part.

Squeaky
What do you mean "look"?

Jay
They think- They told me specifically that- It's a compliment, really.
They think that you look too sweet to play the part of Bob.

Squeaky
Well, get a fucking chisel. Come on, Jay!

Jay
No, no. That's not the way it works. It's just, you're not the right type.

Squeaky
It's a puppet!

Jay
I know that.

(Clip ends from "Jay Johnson: The Two & Only!" – 2007)

Bob

And I was just - I was hired. And then they needed somebody to do Chuck.
So they got Jay. And he was okay. I would rather have an actor, you know?
But he was okay.

(Montage begins from SOAP – 1977 - 1981)

Chuck
Bless you.

Bob
Big ones…
A person can't get a wink of sleep around this house…
Well! Getting a little on the side, huh?...
Turn the page, you dummy…
Well, there's nothing wrong with a nooner…

Chuck
Bob!

Bob
(Choking)
Uhhhh.

Mary Campbell
Burt!

(Montage ends from SOAP – 1977 - 1981)

Bob
Without me he'd be unemployed.

Jay
Jay Sandrich, the director, was really great to me, because he never
treated Bob like a puppet. He was never treated like something other than
just another actor. You would hear him say, "Bob, you need to play a little more
camera left. Bob, you're not in the shot. Bob, you need to find your light Bob,
that line. You flubbed that line."You know? "Jay, you're perfect. Bob, you flubbed
your line." And, I guess it was kind of funny for people to hear. But I understood
that. That was code that I could accept really fast. I could accept that and
work with it. That, it really was as much of a hybrid character as ever had been done.
So I was Chuck and Chuck was Bob. And Jay Johnson was Chuck and Bob.

(Clip begins from SOAP – 1977)

Bob
You're sick, you know that? You're really sick!
I could have frozen in there. You could have killed me.

(Clip ends from SOAP – 1977)

Jay
They were really clueless about what ventriloquism was until
I got involved. And I was able to tailor what needed to be done a lot of times.
I suggested a lot of things that I got to do on the show, simply because I knew that
my survival on the show depended on how many different ways I could be used
on that show. Cause, otherwise, I've see characters be written in until
- And then be written out. And written in, written out. And I was supposed to be
there for seven shows and I stayed for four years.

(Clip begins from SOAP – 1977)

Grapefruit
What's the matter, Jody? You look upset.

Jody Dallas
I'd like to talk to Chuck.

Grapefruit
Oh, how about talking to me? I'm in season. Sweet, just like Bob.

Jody
No, no. I understand- I don't believe this! I'm having a conversation with a
grapefruit here. Chuck? Chuck, look, it's food. Chuck, see? Watch. It's just food.

Grapefruit
Grrrr.

(Clip ends from SOAP – 1977)

Jay
Yeah. It was a difficult and wonderful and challenging and a new experience all
at once when I started doing that on "Soap".

(Clip begins from SOAP – 1977)

Bob
Okay, okay, okay I got it. It's, uh- It's, uh- Red? It's round. It's an apple!

Chuck
Yes!

Danny Dallas
This is amazing!

(Clip ends from SOAP – 1977)

Tom Ladshaw
Jay is not only one of the most technically proficient vents working. He's also
one of the nicest guys. One of the cleverest. And it's interesting if you ever
have the opportunity to hear him lecture on ventriloquism. He's actually
quite the educator as well. I had the good fortune to see his one man show
on Broadway. And I can tell you Jay knocked them dead and got a standing
ovation. And again that's one more way that Jay Johnson's doing his part,
and ventriloquism's profile is getting raised again.

It's Old School ? Paul Winchell

Kelly Asbury
The first ventriloquist to be featured on "The Ed Sullivan Show" was a very young,
energetic Paul Winchell, with this new little brash puppet named Jerry Mahoney.

(Clip begins from Ed Sullivan's "Toast of the Town" – 1948)

Ed Sullivan
When I was a little boy about your size...

Jerry Mahoney
Uh-huh?

Ed Sulivan
And I had a headache...

Jerry
-yeah?

Ed Sullivan
My father used to blow through one ear and he always told me it blew
the headache out the other. It works, too.

Jerry
This guy's smoking seaweed.

Paul Winchell
Now, wait. The man knows what he's talking about.

Jerry
He does?

Paul
Well, sure. Let him try it.

Jerry
All right, I'll try anything once. Go ahead, Ed. Hee, hee. Do it again.
Hee, hee. Now you try it on your side.

Paul
All right.
Jerry
One good one now. Ow!

Paul
Well? How's the headache?

Jerry
It's much worse.

Ed Sullivan
I don't know why it is, it always worked for me.

Jerry
It works for you?

Paul
That's what he said.

Ed Sulliavn
Always worked for me.

Jerry
Uh-huh. Can I see your ear?

Ed Sullivan
Of course.
Jerry
Hi ya, Winch.

Paul
Hi Jerry.

Ed Sullivan
Awe, common now. I'm trying to help you out!
A wise guy, huh?

(Clip ends from Ed Sullivan's "Toast of the Town" – 1948)

Tom Ladshaw
While Paul originally started out, really geared towards adults, he kind of
morphed into a children's ventriloquist. And he had certainly crossover appeal as well.
But kids loved him. And let's face it, he had Saturday morning shows eventually.
And shows geared specifically towards kids.

Kelly Asbury
He went on all sorts of TV shows until he had his own. "The Paul Winchell/
JerryMahoney Show". "Winchell Mahoney Time". "Circus Time with
Paul Winchell & Jerry Mahoney". He had several television shows over
the years. Extremely, extremely popular ventriloquist in the fifties.
And a children's performer like no other.

(Clip begins from "The Paul Winchell & Jerry Mahoney Show" – 1953)

Jerry Mahoney
Gee, Winch, you know I seen you at the theatre tonight?

Paul Winchell
Oh, you did?

Jerry
Oh boy, are you an actor! "Ah, then the moon is not created. The starlight
dancing on the sea. We did not meet. We did not kiss." Boy you was
great! A toast to Winchell! And some bread for Mahoney.

Paul
No you don't.

Jerry
No you don't. You know the part that I liked?

Paul
What?

Jerry
When you took Viveca's earring.

Paul
Yeah.

Jerry
And she took your stick pin.

Paul
Yeah.

Jerry
I'll take some bread.

Paul
Here- No you don't.

Jerry
A roll?

Paul
No rolls.

Jerry
A cracker?

Paul
No cracker!

Jerry
A little crumb?

Paul
No little crumb! Now will you stop this reaching?
What's the matter with you? Don't you have a tongue?

Jerry
Well certainly, but my arm reaches better.

(Clip ends from "The Paul Winchell & Jerry Mahoney Show" – 1953)

Tom Ladshaw
Paul Winchell had a very difficult childhood. He came up under less than ideal.
Apparently, he had a somewhat domineering and/or abusive mother.
Unfortunately he was stricken with polio when he was young. While he was in
bed recovering, he sent off for information on how to become a ventriloquist.
And he devoured the little ten-cent pamphlet. Developed these imaginary
characters to help him cope.

Burt Dubrow
He was a stutterer. He was born with polio. He had a lot to overcome. But
you know, he was a man who, when all was said and done, became a singer,
a dancer and a ventriloquist. All things that he never thought
in a million years he'd become.

Tom Ladshaw
I think really he's one of those people who overcame adversity through
ventriloquism. It was truly therapeutic for him in that it gave him a way to
deal with the day-to-day adversity of his real life.

Kelly Asbury
A lot of Paul Winchell's work is lost. Um, there's a few clips you can see here
and there. And when you see them it's amazing that there's no special effects.
There's no special - There's no special effects of any kind.
It's all Paul Winchell and his amazing choreography. There is no other one.

(Clip begins from "The Paul Winchell & Jerry Mahoney Show" – 1953)

Knucklehead Smiff
(Singing)
There is no other life.

Paul Winchell
(Singing)
No life in which he's fonder.

Knucklehead
Makes me flip the gyp that's in my soul.

Paul
No cares. No strings. His heart has wings.

Knucklehead
Hey, oh, I'm so fancy free,
I'm off to wander way out yonder.

Paul
It's just a gyp. So take a tip.

Knucklehead
I'm just a lonely gypsy, a little ipsy gypsy, and you'll be ipsy tipsy, you'll sing
a happy little song, you'll find you're never going wrong, start slow and
every time you do, and every day you'll find you're way.

Paul
He's right! He's right! Go, go, here. Go, go, here, here. Go, go. Hey, hey.

Knucklehead
Hey, that's the gypsy.

Paul
Ipsy flipsy.

Paul
Hipsy, gypsy.

Knucklehead
Feeling, feeling. Hey, this is,

Paul
My song.

(Clip ends from "The Paul Winchell & Jerry Mahoney Show" – 1953)

Jimmy Nelson
Innovative. He did things that none of us ever thought we could do.

Kelly Asbury
Paul Winchell really was determined, as he said to get the dummy off his knees.
He knew if he wanted to set himself apart from what people usually
associated with ventriloquists, the little wooden dummy on a ventriloquist's knee,
he had to change something.

Burt Dubrow
I think what made Paul Winchell unique. Well there were so many things.
But, certainly as an actor, he acted better than anybody. Which made
him a great ventriloquist. Which made him believable.
Which made those characters believable.

(Clip begins from "The Paul Winchell & Jerry Mahoney Show" – 1953)

Jerry Mahoney
Uh, that picture don't look nothing like it.

Paul Winchell
Like what?

Jerry
Your thumb.

Paul
I'm not painting my thumb.

Jerry
Oh. Well then what is it?

Paul
Well what would you call it?

Jerry
Oh no. I'm not gonna get my mouth washed out with soap.

Paul
It happens to be a painting of an apple.

Jerry
Oh, heaven help the worms on a night like this. Gee whiz, Winch. This is silly.

Paul
Silly? Well.

Jerry
Just because Mary Ellen likes a fellow who can paint that
doesn't mean you gotta paint too.

Paul
Jerry, you just don't understand these things. Now, the right way to
look at it is to stand away from it.

Jerry
Yeah, the further the better.

(Clip ends from "The Paul Winchell & Jerry Mahoney Show" – 1953)

Burt Dubrow
Paul was. Went through life as a very, very frustrated man. He never thought
he was as good as he was. He was insecure. Like most performers,
maybe a little more than most. He had a rough time getting through life.

(Clip begins from "The Paul Winchell & Jerry Mahoney Show" – 1953)

Paul
Hey? Hey, what's going on around here? Hey! Jerry! How come I'm so small?

Jerry
Because the shoe has turned and has the worm on the other foot.
That's why, you little dummy!

Paul
Oh, wait a second.

Jerry
Keep quiet! I want to take a good look at you.

(Clip ends from "The Paul Winchell & Jerry Mahoney Show" – 1953)

Kelly Asbury
He's got a multi-faceted legacy. But it's sort of a secret legacy. As with most stories about ventriloquists, that's a little poignant, a little bittersweet to me, that no one knows who Paul Winchell is anymore.

(Clip begins from "The Paul Winchell & Jerry Mahoney Show" – 1953)

Crow
Caw, caw.

Paul
(Singing)
You see me in the snow and in the rain.

Jerry
(Singing)
And all because he hasn't got a brain.

Crow
You said it.

Paul
I'm full of straw, my clothes are made of patches.

Crow
Caw, caw.

Jerry
And furthermore, he's got the head to match it.

Paul
Oh, here, here boy. Well I was put here for a purpose. Well I was put here for the sparrows and the pigeons and the crows.

Jerry
Yep. You're for the birds.

(Clip ends from "The Paul Winchell & Jerry Mahoney Show" – 1953)

It's Old School ? Señor Wences

Kelly Asbury
Senor Wences was, like his fellow Spaniard Salvador Dali, was a surrealist.

(Clip begins from Ed Sullivan's "Toast of the Town" – 1950's)

Wences
Oh no, no, no. Very confusing music.

Johnny
Difficult.

Wences
I say difficult?

Johnny
Yes.

Wences
Yes.

Johnny
Very easy.

Wences
I say very difficult, Johnny?

Johnny
Yes.

Wences
Yes.

Johnny
Easy.

Wences
I say difficult?

Johnny
Yes.

Wences
Yes. Say difficult.

Johnny
Difficult.

Wences
Louder.

Johnny
Difficult.

Wences
Louder.

Johnny
Difficult.

Wences
Louder.

Johnny
Difficult.

Wences
Louder.

Johnny
Difficult.

Wences
Good. Very difficult.

Johnny
For you. For me, very easy.

(Clip ends from Ed Sullivan's "Toast of the Town" – 1950's)

Norm Nielsen
Wences was a surrealist because it was inside him. That's the way he interpreted
things. He became almost childlike. When Wences would mimic somebody in
class and the teacher found out about it she would punish him. And she would make
him fill all the inkwells. And he didn't like that idea at all. So he was doing a
rather messy job and he got ink smeared on his first finger and his thumb.
And he looked at that and he thought, "Oh my God, that looks like a mouth."
And he put two dots above it and they became the eyes. And he was doing
this for the teacher in the class and the whole class was howling. Johnny was
a little child that he was speaking to as if you would see a child talking to a doll.

Tom Ladshaw
Senor Wences was traveling to Chicago area. He had a job to do there. And
The train arrived and there had been a shift in baggage. In the baggage car.
And Pedro's body was horribly crushed.

Kelly
All that was left was the head. Well, Senor Wences had to go onstage that night.
And he needed money. And he needed to work. And if he didn't have a
dummy, he didn't have an act. So, somehow he got the idea to put this head in a box.

Norm
And he showed it to the stage manager. And the stage manager said,
"That ugly thing? If you use that," he says. "You're gonna be fired." And Wences,
he didn't know not to do it. So he took the box out on stage and he did
Pedro in the box. And created such a sensation.

Kelly
And the audience howled. He was hired to come back and do it again.
And this sort of classic, odd, surreal act was invented. And it took him through
his career for probably seventy more years. He did the very same act.
Very same thing. It really was a phenomenon. And one of the happiest
accidents in certainly show business history.

Jay Johnson
So disaster is the mother of invention, isn't it? You know, Pedro is the classic.
The head in the box. It always will be.

(Clip begins from "The Ed Sullivan Show" – 1960's)

Wences
Hello, my friend!

Pedro
[Muffled] I'm not ready yet.

Wences
Not yet. No?

Pedro
No, no, no, no.

Weñces
Are you tired?

Pedro
No.

Weñes
No?

Pedro
No.

Weñes
Sokay?

Pedro
So right.

Weñes
All right.

(Clip begins from "The Ed Sullivan Show" – 1960's)

Kelly Asbury
He had performed for years, traveling all over. All over the world, really.
But it was The Ed Sullivan Show that became his venue and it's where he gained
most of his fame. He was a brilliant ventriloquist and his lips never moved.
And he was a magician. He could make Johnny smoke and blow smoke rings.
To this day no oneknows how he did that. Magicians don't know how he did that.
He just was an artist. And he found a venue on The Ed Sullivan Show.
Johnny would get this huge applause and it was as if this other actor was
coming onstage. It's just part of Senor Wences' amazing artistry.

Tom Ladshaw
So he had these various talents and he put them together in this bizarre mixture
that probably know one else in the world ever would have come up with.
And today we describe it as surrealist in nature.

Jimmy Nelson
He could juggle, which he did in his act. He could draw caricatures.
He was an all-around performer, not just a ventriloquist.

Norm Nielsen
His juggling was absolutely incredible. His plate spinning and juggling.
And the way he incorporated Pedro. You know, he would be spinning
a plate over the box and Pedro's door would be open.

Jay Johnson
And he says, "What do you think?" And Pedro says, "Pretty good!" And there's
this moment of brilliant timing where it's still spinning and the door's open and
Pedro says, "Shut the door!" Because he did not want the plate to fall on him.
It was the most brilliant moment I've ever seen on a stage. You know?
Cause it was- The timing on it was perfect. Just long enough for Pedro to
look up, be concerned, understand, grasp the situation and
tell him to close the door. It was great.

Norm
When Senor Wences has his 103rd birthday, three days later he went to sleep and
didn't wake up. Out in front of my door was a steamer trunk and a valise. We
opened the valise and I couldn't believe it. It was Senor Wences' entire act. And
in the steamer trunk were many, many puppets and heads that he had made
himself. So we have all of his things in this case that you saw in the living room.
And we're so proud of them. And we are really happy that we can share this with you.

Jay
There's a street right side of, now it's the David Letterman theatre.
But it's the old Ed Sullivan Theatre.

Tom
It's on the corner of 54th and Broadway. And that little area now,
that stretches to the backstreet, is known as Senor Wences Way.

Jay
Because he did so many shots on The Ed Sullivan Show, which is that theatre
right there, they named the street after him.

Jimmy
Every time you saw his act you didn't care if you had seen it before.
You wanted to see that same act over and over again. Because it was so good.

Tom
He is one of the few ventriloquists that transcended popular culture, in
that there was a time when you could walk down the street and say,
"So right?" And anyone would answer, "So right."

(Clip begins from "The Ed Sullivan Show" – 1960's)

Weñces
Pedro?

Pedro
(Muffled) I'm not ready yet.

Weñces
Not yet!

Pedro
No, no.

Weñces
Take it easy. Take it easy, please. Are you ready?

Pedro
No.

Weñces
Sokay?

Pedro
So right.

Weñces
All right, that's good.

(Clip ends from "The Ed Sullivan Show" – 1960's)

It's Old School ? Jimmy Nelson

Tom Ladshaw
I was a child of the early sixties. Watched a lot of television. Particularly on
Saturday mornings. But I guess the difference between me and a lot of
the other kids was that on Saturday mornings I suffered through the cartoons to
get to the commercials. Because I was waiting for Jimmy Nelson to come on
Danny O'Day and Farfel. For me, Danny O'Day and Farfel were it.

(Clip begins from Nestlés Quik Commercial)

Farfel
We got 74 cases and 3,000 quarts.

Jimmy Nelson
74 cases and 3,000 quarts? What kind of fuel is that?

Danny O'Day
Nestle's Quik Milk. Natch. What'd you think?

Jimmy
Danny, you're crazy.

Danny
I'm crazy about chocolatey Quik in milk. You bet! I won't go anywhere
without it, you know? Five, four, three, two-

(Clip ends from Nestlés Quik Commercial)

Tom Ladshaw
But the funny thing is, at the time I didn't quite get Jimmy Nelson's role along
side them. I thought they were these couple of magical puppets that could speak.

Kelly Asbury
Every ventriloquist today had either a Danny O'Day doll or a Paul Winchell/
Jerry Mahoney doll. And they had Jimmy Nelson's instructional album.
So many people working today go back to that.

Jeff Dunham
Jimmy Nelson's album was the perfect teacher for me. Both of them.
The first, "Instant Ventriloquism" and then the follow-up, the blue one.
I think it was great because he hit upon a very simple way of
teaching and learning ventriloquism, that anybody could follow
and understand.

Jimmy Nelson
I said to myself, well there had been books on ventriloquism. There had been
instructions. There was a school for awhile. All very complicated. I thought if I
could put together a record album with Danny O'Day on it and Farfel on it
and myself. And the three of us talking to each other. And talking to the people
listening to this album, maybe we could make it more interesting.

Jeff
On the album he's just a delight. Just like he is in person. So, it came across.
When I met him for the first time, I'm like, this is the same guy that's on the
album. He's no different. He's this sweet man that is very funny with
his characters. The voices are great. And it made me realize that what
I'm about to learn is going to be fun.

(Soundtrack begins from "Instant Ventriloquism")

Jimmy
Uh, Danny?

Danny
Yes, Nelson?

Jimmy
It seems to me that if I could teach you how to be a ventriloquist.

Danny
Yeah?

Jimmy
I could teach just about anybody.

Danny
That's a heck of a way to start this record, Nelson.
Look, isn't this supposed to be simplified ventriloquism for the beginner?

Jimmy
Right.

Danny
I'm way past that stage. I haven't been a beginner for years.

Jimmy
I know that, Danny. But you've been a dummy all your life. And I...

Danny
Geee! Watch your language, Nelson.

Jimmy
Sorry. Look, if I teach ventriloquism to you, and if you ask questions
as we go along, I think it'd make a more interesting record
for the beginner. And you'll be able to learn ventriloquism
in a surprisingly short time.

(Soundtrack ends from "Instant Ventriloquism")

Tom Ladshaw
On the original Jimmy Nelson album, he espouses the philosophy of
sound substitution. Using, for instance, the letter D for B. And what
Jimmy always says and says to this day is...

Jimmy
You say D, but you think B. So it doesn't come out D, but it comes out B.
So it's a softer sound and it sounds much more like a B than a D.

Tom
So instead of saying basketball, you would say dasketdall. But you think
basketball. So, with the lips in the proper position and the teeth in
the proper position and the tongue in the proper position,
instead of it sounding like dasketdall, it should sound like basketball.

Jimmy
You can do that with all the letters of the alphabet that are difficult.
And I think that's one of the things that ventriloquists who
got anything out of my albums picked up on.

Tom
That's what so many of us in the early sixties learned with, was that album.
And I all but wore that album out. And I eventually got it.
I understood Jimmy's role in it and how important it was,
which I didn't initially. And from there I was hooked.

Jay Johnson
And for me, what I found watching Jimmy Nelson work, was attitude.

(Clip begins from Ed Sullivan's "Toast of the Town" – 1951)

114

Jimmy
Repeat after me. Ven.

Danny
Ven.

Jimmy
Tril.

Danny
Tril.

Jimmy
O.

Danny
O.

Jimmy
Quist.

Danny
Quist.

Jimmy
Ventriloquist.

Danny
So how come you can say it and I can't?

Jimmy
Look, what are you going to do for them?

Danny
Where did you get the jacket? Gee! Looks like something
from the seat cover of your car, doesn't it?

Jimmy
It's not.

Danny
No?

Jimmy
No.

(Clip ends from Ed Sullivan's "Toast of the Town" – 1951)

Jay Johnson
And that's really where my comedy comes with Bob, I think, is attitude.

(Clip begins from the Comedy and Magic Club, Redondo Beach, CA)

Bob
I don't care. I don't care, Jay. I don't care. I don't need the job.
You need the job, I don't need the job, Jay. You need me, I do not need you, Jay.

Jay
I need you?

Bob
You need me.

Jay
Really?

Bob
Yeah. Without me, you're going to be standing in unemployment, talking to your hand.

Jay
Okay. Yeah, you know what? I think. I think I have more job opportunities.
You have limited job...

Bob
Not me man, I got another job, Jay! I got another job, Jaaay!

(Clip ends from the Comedy and Magic Club, Redondo Beach, CA)

Jay Johnson
The economy of words. The economy of attitudes. The difference. There was
no question between Jimmy Nelson and Danny O'Day. There just-
There were two distinct people with two distinct attitudes. With lives.
I mean, it really- The essence of ventriloquism
is that separation. And he's that good to do that, even today.

(Clip begins from Ed Sullivan's "Toast of the Town" – 1952)

Danny O'Day
Hiya, Charlie? By George, you're my favorite bartender.

Jimmy Nelson
Look, when you were backstage you didn't have any...

Danny
I certainly did. And I feel veeeery good about it. Takes me back to my school days.

Jimmy
Never mind your school days.

Danny
I like a little drink, if you don't mind.

Jimmy
No more drink.

(Clip ends from Ed Sullivan's "Toast of the Town" – 1952)

Kelly Asbury
In the early fifties. Very early fifties, he was a regular spokesperson
for Texaco on Milton Berle's Texaco Star Theatre.

Tom Ladshaw
We didn't have commercials on television then the way we have them today.
As a rule an hour show might have a five to ten minute commercial right
smack in the middle of the show. And it was live, as the rest of the show was live.

(Clip begins from Texaco Star Theatre – 1952)

Jimmy
Television's better than ever.

Danny
Oh, I am sharp today.

Jimmy
What do you mean, sharp today?

Danny
Yes.

Jimmy
You know, your car gives sharp performance everyday when
you fill the tank with Texaco Fire Chief.

Danny
I knew we'd get around to this sooner or later.

(Clip ends from Texaco Star Theatre – 1952)

Jimmy
The people at Texaco wanted a ventriloquist to do their commercial.
They caught my act at Radio City Music Hall. And said that's fine. That's what
we want. New Year's Day 1952, I started on the Milton Berle Texaco Star Theatre,
doing the commercials half way through the hour show. Now, the commercial
ran for five minutes. So we didn't just do the product, we used some of the
guests from the show. And they would work with me in the commercial.

(Clip begins from Texaco Star Theatre – 1952)

Jimmy
Now look, Danny, if you don't behave yourself, I won't ask Ronald Reagan
to give you a part in the picture.

Danny
Who cares? I'm better looking than he is anyway.

Jimmy
Better looking than Ronald Reagan?

Danny
Yeah.

Jimmy
Why Danny, Ronald Reagan is a very handsome man.

Danny
Are you kidding? You think he's handsome?

Jimmy
Yeah.

Danny
You hear that, Humphrey? He thinks that- How are you? You
think that Ronald Reagan... Ha, ha, ha... Timber!

Jimmy
Hiya, Ronnie, old pal.

Ronald Regan
Hello Jimmy. Hiya Danny.

Tom Ladshaw
It wasn't until he was doing those constant barrage commercials for Nestle's,
that he really pretty much became a household name.

(Series of Nestlés Quik Commercial clips begins)

V. O.
Let's get with Jimmy Nelson & Danny O'Day.

Danny O'Day
Now I'm gonna do a little song called "The Chocolate Rock."
Made it up out of my head.

Farfel
You certainly are.

Danny
Why you!

Jimmy Nelson
Just sing, Danny.

V.O.
Here's racing driver Danny O'Day!

Danny
Hey Nelson! Hurry up!

Jimmy
Okay, Danny. I'll check the oil, water and gas.

Danny
Gas? I run on Nestlés Quik. Chochlatey New Quik full of vitamins.

Farfel
It's fun to make as quick as instant.

Danny
Are you all warmed up?

Farfel
Yes.

Danny
Show them your stuff!

Farfel
Oh…

Danny
N-E-S-T-L-E-S... Nestle makes the very best.

Farfel
Chocolate.

(Series of Nestlés Quik commercial clips ends)

Kelly Asbury
Jimmy Nelson really has two legacies. On a broad scale, his legacy is as one
of the greatest television pitch men of all time. He really is part of an era of people

who did television commercials, who did them live. And they were showmen. And he was a real pro at it. His other legacy is also as a very generous guy in teaching young ventriloquists. Up and coming ventriloquists over the years who were interested in the art form. From his records that he made that were instructional records. So Jimmy is a mentor as much as a legend in his own right.

Jay Johnson
Jimmy taught us more than he knows. But we're grateful that he taught us how to be- How to be nice guys and gentlemen. And how to spread the word on how to be a good performer. He still is the best.

(Musical clip begins from Ed Sullivan's "Toast of the Town" – 1950)

Danny
Heart and soul.

Humphrey Higsbye
So M.

Danny
M.

Humphrey
I said M-O.

Danny
He said M-O.

Humphrey
M-O-P

Danny
M-O-P

Humphrey
M-O-P-P

Danny
M-O-P-P

Humphrey
Mop.

Danny
Mop.

Humphrey
Mop. M-O-P-P, Mop, Mop, Mop, Mop. Ragg Mop.

Danny
Da di da da da da.

Humphrey
Ragg Mop.

Danny
Da di da da da da.

Humphrey
Ragg Mop.

Danny
Da di da da da da.

Humphrey
Ragg Mop.

Danny
Da di da da da da.

Humphrey
Ragg Mop.

Danny
Da di da da da da.

Humphrey
R-A-G-G

Danny
M-O-P-P

Jimmy nelson
A

Danny
A

Jimmy
I said A-B.

Danny
A-B

Ed Sulivan
Great.

(Musical clip ends from Ed Sullivan's "Toast of the Town" – 1950)

Jimmy
When you're in show business you never retire. I mean as long as
the telephone rings. When it stops, then you say, "I'm retired".

It's Old School ? Edgar Bergen

Kelly Asbury
Edgar Bergen's considered the great master in this day and age. Certainly, his
great accomplishment, and it's really a testament to how well-rounded and believable
his characters were, was because he was able to gain such giant super stardom.
And that's a testament to the voice acting. That's a testament to the writing
and the overall performance quality that Bergen would put into his act.

(Clip begins from Charlie McCarthy Detective – 1939)

Edgar Bergen
How do you do?

Charlie McCarthy
Why, you gave me quite a stir.

Edgar
Yes.

Charlie
I didn't expect you.

Edgar
Is that so?

Charlie
Yeah.

Edgar
Well, I'd like to buy six hot dogs.

Charlie
Yeah?

Edgar
And four lemonades.

Charlie
Is that so?

Edgar
Yes.

Charlie
Did you hear that? Business is buzzing, Gravy.

Gravy
Yes sir! Buzzing right along.

Charlie
Yeah. Buzzing right along, yes sir.

Edgar
Well, how much will it cost me?

Charlie
Oh. Six hot dogs and four lemonades. Six... four.. How much is that, Gravy?

Gravy
Six hot dogs and four lemonades?

(Clip ends from Charlie McCarthy Detective – 1939)

Kelly Asbury
On Vaudeville, Charlie was really dressed like a little newsboy. With a little
sweater and a little soft cloth hat. Edgar Bergen upgraded his act when he went
to supper clubs. And he wanted to make Charlie more sophisticated.

Dr, David Golblatt
One of the great, ingenious ideas was putting these guys in tuxedos. You know,
that was one of the things. Because that gave a certain kind of sophistication to
an extreme unsophisticated act. And that became a kind of emblem, you know,
for that act. And I think when they were in tuxedos, that was,
in some sense, the best of the best of those acts.

Kelly Asbury
It took, who could have ever guessed? I mean, then he became sort of
the toast of New York.

(Clip begins from Letter of Introduction – 1938)

Honey
Beer?

Edgar Bergen
Thank you.

Charlie McCarthy
Uh, uh, uh, Bergen.

Edgar
Quiet. Can't you see I'm trying to drink?

Charlie
Yes, but Honey, Honey didn't give Charlie, Charlie any beer.

Honey
I beg your pardon. I'll get you some.

Charlie
Alright.

Honey
Here you are, Charlie dear.

Charlie
Oh! Last but not least, I thank you. I, uh… I, I, I…

Edgar
Too much beer isn't good for little boys.

Charlie
Too much beer?

Edgar
No.

Charlie
Uh-huh. Well, you certainly took care of that.

(Clip ends from Letter of Introduction – 1938)

Kelly Asbury
Prior to Charlie's incarnation with the top hat and monocle,
Edgar Bergen did do several short films, even before the radio success.
With he and Charlie, for the Vitaphone Corporation. They were just
little short films that played before movies.

Tom Ladshaw
He created, in Charlie McCarthy, a living, breathing character.
Charlie's not a puppet. And he's not a puppet, even a puppet with a personality.
He's a person. It's not Edgar Bergen and his dummy, Charlie McCarthy.
It's Edgar Bergen and Charlie McCarthy.

(Series of clips from the short films begins)

Edgar Bergen
Is it all right if I leave you alone?

Charlie Mc Carthy
All right? It's marvelous. Well now that we're alone, tell me, toots.
What do you really think of me?

Charlie
Easy, Professor. Easy.

Young Woman
So brave.

Charlie
So what? You know I'm quite a cutter-upper myself, you know?
Hot chee tot chee tot chee.

Young Woman
I get it.

Charlie
Oh. Well, will you come down out of the stratosphere and park the lips
under the schnozola?

(Series of clips from the short films ends)

Kelly Asbury
Bergen did work hard to create the illusion of life in Charlie. And he wanted
the public to see Charlie as a real boy. And he was very successful at that.
He would do magazine interviews. And they'd have photographs of Charlie and Edgar flying
their plane together. Edgar Bergen was an avid pilot.
And he would have a picture of himself and Charlie.

Tom Ladshaw
Most importantly, always making Charlie appear to be a living, breathing
character in the picture. Not just the puppet on the guy's arm.

Kelly Asbury
Anything he could do for the public to see this as really a father and son,
he did it. I think some of the public even took that further years later.
And they thought that he really did live that way, but he didn't.
It was all part of the publicity. He was really a pro at publicity.

Tom Ladshaw
And I think that's why Edgar Bergen transcended what he did.
Because Charlie McCarthy transcended what he was.

Jimmy Nelson
Charlie got more fan mail than Edgar ever did.

Kelly Asbury
Again, the whole point of ventriloquism is to create the illusion of life.

Tom Ladshaw
And Bergen, perhaps more than anyone else, did that in Charlie
and Mortimer and Effie and his other friends.

Kelly Asbury
Edgar Bergen died on September 30th, 1978 at Caesar's Place. He was performing...

Tom Ladshaw
...with Andy Williams. And he was performing a couple of shows a night.
And the last night of the run he did his regular act. Got his regular
standing ovation. And as it's oft been told, he said every vaudeville act
must have a beginning and an end. And that time has come for me, so I'll pack
my jokes and my little friends and say goodbye. And he went off stage...

Kelly Asbury
...went to bed that night. And quietly died in his sleep. He was as big a star as,
there really ever was. And sadly, that's been somewhat lost to time, because we
don't see a lot of ventriloquism. And we don't get a lot of introduction to it
on television or in the movies anymore.

(Clip begins from Letter of Introduction – 1938)

Edgar Bergen
Charlie, come on! We've got to get out of here!

Charlie McCarthy
What's that? I thought the landlady gave you till Monday to dig up the rent.
Achoo! What are they trying to do, smoke us out of here?

Edgar
No, the building's on fire!

Charlie
Wow! Let's get out of here.

(Clip ends from Letter of Introduction – 1938)

Dr. David Goldblatt
The origin of the dummy is the ventriloquist. But in some way,
the origin of the ventriloquist is also the dummy. Because Edgar Bergen
would not be Edgar Bergen without Charlie McCarthy.

Where Do Dummies Go When They Die?

Lisa Sweasy
This is Vent Haven Museum. Vent Haven is the only museum in the world dedicated
to the art of ventriloquism. It was originally a private collection, assembled
by a man named W.S. Berger. His full name was William Shakespeare Berger.

Kelly Asbury
He loved ventriloquism all his life. From the early 1900's he was a fan
from vaudeville. And for 46 years he lived in this house on Maple Drive
in Fort Mitchell, where he collected...

Tom Ladshaw
...anything and everything to do pertaining to ventriloquism. Or, as he coined
the term, ventriloquiana. In fact he called himself, the very first ventriloquarian.

Lisa Sweasy
So, today we have 726 ventriloquial figures. And we have Mr. Berger's letter
collection, which is probably around a quarter of a million letters.
And we also have about 10,000 photographs. We have scripts and playbills,
posters. Just about anything you can imagine related to ventriloquism.

Kelly Asbury
The first time I went to the Vent Haven Museum, I was working on my book.
I was following Jimmy Nelson around. The first impression is sort

of shocking, because you see all these faces staring back at you. Rooms full of ventriloquist's dummies. You're taken aback at first. And I started realizing that in show business at one time or another.

Tom Ladshaw
The museum to me, is still a very personal experience every time I walk in it. I see something different every time. I experience different emotions. I look at pictures on the wall and if I'm familiar with the ventriloquist, it brings back verypleasant memories. That's part of the fun of being a collector and a historian. It's going after these stories. Finding out about these people. Because one thing I've learned over the many, many, many trips to the museum is that every single piece, every figure, every loose head, every photograph, every poster, every playbill. It's all got a fascinating story behind it.

Is This the End of Ventriloquism?

Jeff Dunham
Walter, people keep asking me, "Do you think ventriloquism is a dying art form?"

Walter
It was never living. It's always been on a stinking pacemaker.

Jeff
No. It's been great. It's been great for us.

Walter
Yeah, whatever. You, maybe. We're still stuck in the stinking suitcase.

Jeff
Okay. But people are accepting it as a legitimate form of entertainment now.

Walter
He lives in this world. No one else knows what the hell he's talking about.

Jay Johnson
I don't think ventriloquism is a dying art. But I have no idea where it's headed.

Burt Dubrow
I'm sorry to say, yes. I think it is a dying art form.

Jeff
I think if ventriloquism is going to progress as an art or a form of comedy, people have to change. They have to do be doing an act now that's contemporary, be it the material or the presentation. Does that mean that the little wooden dummy will go away? No. I just think that, that people have to keep pushing the envelope with the characters. And come up with things that appeal to the audiences. And material that is fresh.

Vonda Van Dyke
I mean it was vaudeville for goodness sakes. It's ages ago.

Kurley Q
Yeah, so none of us will be able to come alive again.

(Clip begins of Arthur Prince and Jim – 1934)

Jim
If I die tonight, they won't know who I belonged to.

125

Arthur Prince
Well what happened after that?

Jim
I don't remember anymore, sir. All I remembered when I opened me eyes was
that there was an angel standing over me, sir. All dressed in white.

(Clip ends of Arthur Prince and Jim – 1934)

Tom Ladshaw
Even Paul Winchell understood and could see the light at the end of the tunnel.
Or maybe it was the dark at the end of the tunnel, when he said, Everything
can talk." And it can. When a child goes to Disney World and he sees
totem poles speaking, again, how is a ventriloquist going to compete with that?
They don't even need a ventriloquist.

Jeff Dunham
There's some great avenues for this art that are beyond, different from just
straight comedy. So I think it will always be here. I hope it will always be here.
I hope it doesn't just die away. And I think the more kids that
get interested in it the better.

Lisa Sweasy
I certainly think it's got two lives. There's the archaic version of ventriloquism.
The history. Particularly the pre-TV history. A lot of people just don't know that.
And aren't particularly interested in knowing it. And do perceive it as archaic
and outdated. But since Sullivan- And now, you know, with the internet. And clips
of everything online. And everything that's ever been on television you can
almost find online anymore. People are seeing ventriloquists. I mean, there's
Jeff Dunham. There's Jay Johnson's show. There are people who are doing this.
So I don't think it's in any peril, as far as dying out forever. But it's an old art form.
It's a vaudevillian thing to do. And yet there are these contemporary people
who put a whole new life on it. So, no. I don't think it's going anywhere.

Mallory Lewis
The simple act of ventriloquism is no longer enough of a parlor trick.

Stevo Schüling
It has a present. It has a past. And it will have a future.

Jimmy Nelson
Boy, if I thought it was dying I really would be very depressed. Well, I know
that it's not dying, because my telephone still rings.

Jay Johnson
But I know it's not a dying art. Because art never dies. Art is an expression.
And we have to stop expressing to kill an art form.

(Clip begins from Jeff Dunham's "Spark of Insanity" tour)

Peanut
Waaaaa.

Jeff Dunham
What are you doing?

Peanut
Peanut-Fu.

Jeff
What happened to Kung-Fu?

Peanut
Can't do Kung-Fu.

Jeff
Why not?

Peanut
'Cause to do Kung-Fu, you gotta be able to use both arms and this
one kinda sucks. Big fancy show like this you outta be able to do both
frickin' arms. Well this one works. What the hell is that?
(Clip ends from Jeff Dunham's "Spark of Insanity" tour)

Jeff
I try and concentrate on what's funny and what makes these characters
believable to the audience. And I think that's- I know that's why they come
back over and over to see the shows.

Tom Ladshaw
If you see Jeff's act from year to year to year, it changes constantly.
It's always updating. Always improving. Always growing. And I think that's
important for an act to stay vital. If you want to stay vital, stay alive,
you have to grow. Jeff's act grows. And I think his characters grow.

(Clip begins from Jeff Dunham's "Spark of Insanity" tour)

Jeff Dunham
Thank you, well ladies and gentleman, now we come to the more serious part
of our show. It wasn't to long ago that I became acquainted with a terrorist.
Now this guy was apparently not an accomplished terrorist. In fact I don't know
if he managed to do anything he set out to do, the only thing I do know
that he managed to do was to blow himself up. Ladies and gentleman
please help me welcome Achmed, the dead terrorist.

Achmed
Ha, ha, ha, ha. Good evenings, infidels. Ha, ha, ha, ha.

Jeff
Good evening, Achmed.

Achmed
Good evening infidel number one. It's good to see you. Ha, ha, ha, ha.

Jeff
So Achmed.

Achmed
Yes.

Jeff
Now you for the folks who might not know, are a suicide bomber.

Achmed
Yes I am, don't stand to close.

Jeff
And if you are a suicide bomber, you've obviously finished your job.

127

Achmed
What?

Jeff
Well, you're dead.

Achmed
No, I'm not. I feel fine.

Jeff
But you're all bone.

Achmed
It's a flesh wound. Silence. I kill you.

Jeff
And I understand that you kill in hopes of later obtaining virgins?

Achmed
Are you kidding me? I'd kill you for a Klondike Bar. Ha, ha, ha, ha.

Jeff
And you're Muslim?

Achmed
No.

Jeff
You're not?

Achmed
No, look at my ass, it says made in China.

Walter
(Off Stage)
They're going to recall you.

Achmed
What is Walter talking about? I don't want to go back to China.

(Clip ends from Jeff Dunham's "Spark of Insanity" tour)

Walter
You know, my first performances were actually a surprise to Jeff. Isn't that correct?

Jeff
Yeah. I thought you'd last, you know, maybe a couple minutes onstage.

Walter
But it was a surprise because everyone knows someone just like me.

Jeff
That's right. Somebody grumpy, cantankerous.

Walter
I was going to say good looking.

Jeff
Oh. Yeah, well. That, as well.

Walter
Yeah. And so I'm like an everyman. Everybody has someone
like me inside them. Yeah.

Jeff
Yeah. And so you were able to do jokes and humor...

Walter
Excuse me?

Jeff
Okay.

Walter
I was able to do jokes and humor that everyone could relate to.

Jeff
Right.

Walter
Shut up.

(Clip begins from Jeff Dunham's "Spark of Insanity" tour)

Walter
I said I go back to the hotel room and get on the Internet.

Jeff
On the computer?

Walter
No on the fuckin' toaster. Because my hairdryer won't run windows.
You truly are a moron.

(Clip ends from Jeff Dunham's "Spark of Insanity" tour)

Walter
Jeff and I started working together in, what was it? The middle 80s?

Jeff
Middle 80s.

Walter
Yeah. His act was so sad at the time. He had some purple little
idiot puppet. It was like a Muppet on crack.

Jeff
That was Peanut.

Walter
I know. That's all he had. And then I came along and made the act much
more hip. And you know, so now he's been a success since I came along.
Been, what? Twenty stinking years?

Jeff
Almost.

Walter
Yeah. Twenty years.

Tom Ladshaw
He has essentially, for all intents and purposes,
transcended ventriloquism itself.

Jimmy Nelson
Jeff had a spark right from the beginning. He had it, as they say.

Fan
I saw him once on TV and I knew I had to see him live. It was amazing.
Oh man. Where he gets those ideas I have no idea. But they were hilarious.
Ventriloquism is amazing. I honestly can't think of anything better.
I mean, with his act. With comedy, it's awesome. He's phenomenal.
You forget that he's... You forget that he's the one actually talking.
It's so real. It amazes me how he can do all those characters.
He can just throw his voice somewhere else
and they come to life.

Jimmy Nelson
Even now, I mean, Jeff is a big personality. A big star in show business.

Fan
It was great. I think it's a new thing. It's a new and upcoming-
He's brought it back again bigger than ever.

Tom Ladshaw
His medium is ventriloquism and he has shown the public that puppets
can be funny. And ventriloquism can be hip.

Fan
Dunham and the puppets. We love him. We love dolls.

Jeff
One of the things I'm proud of now is I guess I am making a mark in the
ventriloquist world. As tiny as it is. I guess when it comes to the history of it,
just because of the DVD and some of the accomplishments, and some of the stuff
in the museum, I guess I'll be remembered as somebody who made some
kind of mark. And I am very happy about that. I'm very proud of that.
This little- This quirky little art has been very good to me. And I've had a load of fun
with it. And I'm not finished yet. And, uh- Yeah. I'm concerned with the history of
ventriloquism and that it does keep going. And that it is an art that stays there
for a while. Cause it's fun. That's all there is to it. It's just goofy fun.

Walter
Hey! Thanks for watching. Here's an hour and a half of your life
you'll never get back. Ha, ha, ha. What an idiot.

www.ingramcontent.com/pod-product-compliance
Lightning Source LLC
LaVergne TN
LVHW081317060426
835509LV00015B/1557